The Game Finder

A Leader's Guide to Great Activities

The Game Finder

A Leader's Guide to Great Activities

by

Annette C. Moore

Venture Publishing, Inc.
State College, PA

The author and publisher caution the professional to be sensitive to the abilities and limitations of the participants. The nature of some activities may not be appropriate for your clients. Professional judgment on your part is required.

Cover Design/Illustrator: Dennis Perry
Production: Bonnie Godbey
Printing and Binding: Thomson-Shore, Inc.

Library of Congress Catalogue Card Number 92-61287
ISBN 0-910251-57-6

"It's fun to have fun,

but you have to know how."

THE CAT IN THE HAT

Dr. Seuss

This book is dedicated to

my dad, the late Joe Cardenuto,

who taught me how to help others have fun,

and who encouraged me to love others; and

to my Father, who supplies that love.

Table Of Contents

Acknowledgements

Many people assisted in making this book a reality. Some contributed specific games or inspired ideas, while others were a source of encouragement. I greatly appreciated the abundant supply of both! While thank you's are in order for too many people to mention, I would like to express special gratitude to the following people.

First, thank you to my Recreation and Park 105 students at Penn State University, who so willingly participated in every class, tried my new games, and came up with some good ones of their own! Secondly, I want to thank my illustrator, Dennis Perry. His involvement in the book has added life to these pages, and friendship to our families. Special thanks to Brad Bates for *Wall Ball* and *Tanks*; to Jen Cline and Jen Haldeman for *Recycling Rangers Relay;* to Nancy Jekubovich for *Cooperative Bean Bag Toss;* to Bob Kurzinger and Laura Emmons for *Human Twister;* to Chuck Murphy for *Inflated Interests;* to Pedro Ruiz for *Bandana Balance* and *Bandana Ball;* to Dave Stragand for *Sunbather's Relay;* to Jeff Witherite for *Licorice Lunacy Race;* and to Will Dingman for *52 Card Pick Up* and for a memorable game of *Bronco Tag.*

My deepest appreciation goes to my family: my husband, Roger, for his unending encouragement and help; and our daughters, Sarah and Marinna, for their enthusiastic support of "Mom's Book." Being a family together is the ultimate in fun!

Introduction

It is with great pleasure that I introduce you to this book. I have enjoyed researching and compiling the activities listed herein. Many books have been written in the last century regarding recreation activities. Pawing through them has been fascinating and encouraging. Though technology may change the types of activities people pursue and the equipment used, some things remain the same. People always have, and always will, need to play. Being able to lead activities that bring a smile to the faces of the players is a very rewarding experience. I'm happy to say lots of smiling was going on through the "testing" of these activities.

But more importantly, and quite sincerely, I have been thinking about *you* as I prepared this book. Granted, I probably don't know you, and we may never meet. But through this book, I hope I am able to encourage you, and provide you with information and activities that will help you as an activity leader. In turn, you will be able to touch people's lives, to encourage them, and to build them up, to have some fun!

As an activity leader, you are in a prestigious position: facilitating fun for folks. For the most part, people come to you expecting to have a good time. They look to you to provide them with the setting, leadership, and activities they need to make their expectations a reality. This leadership handbook has been designed to assist you do just that.

The activities presented here have been selected, "tested," and organized so they will be easy for you to lead, and enjoyable and encouraging for your participants. Whether your group is larger or smaller, younger or older, infinitely mobile or less so, you will find many practical leadership tips and scores of fun activities to get you started.

Nothing can teach you recreation leadership as well as actual experience can. I invite you to review the program planning and leadership tips outlined in the first three chapters. Then, flip to the back of the book, to the Game Finder (beginning on page 181), for a quick index of the games, listed by category. A grid shows what size group, what level of effort, what setting, the amount of time, and if special preparation is needed to play the game. Select an activity you are familiar with, grab a few friends, and get out there and give it a go! The more you lead recreation activities, the more confident and capable you will become.

Have fun!

CHAPTER 1

So You Want To Be An Activity Leader!

Role and Importance of the Activity Leader

In the introduction, I mentioned that the activity leader was a "prestigious position," and I firmly believe this. As an activity leader, you are in a position to help people feel good about themselves. When people feel good about themselves, they are more able to feel good about those around them, and about the world in which they live.

For those of you who work with children, you have a tremendous opportunity to encourage and mold the next generation of world leaders, scholars, workers, and family members. What an impact your smiling face and caring attitude can have on these young people!

For those of you who work with adults, your opportunities to encourage individuals are equally great. In fact, your opportunities are ever increasing. As the American population ages, more services will be needed for older clientele. Social recreation provides enjoyable activities in a social setting for adults, as well.

People of all ages benefit from exercise, mental stimulation, social interactions, and just plain fun! Regardless of the age group you are able to work with, you are in a prestigious position as an activity leader. By combining well-prepared, well-run programs, with a sincere concern for others, you can have a positive influence on many people's lives. And that, I believe, is what life is all about!

Qualities of an Effective Leader

To be an effective activities leader, you will need to possess or develop certain basic leadership qualities. The first, perhaps obvious, one is *a sincere desire to work with people.* If you do not enjoy working with people, helping them to have fun and learn new things, perhaps you should consider another area of employment. I have seen adults (young as well as older) in charge of groups of young people, who obviously hated what they were doing. (Needless to say, the participants were having a mediocre to miserable time. What a waste of a potentially positive experience.) The purpose of our programs should be to help others develop individually, and as positive members of our society. As an activity leader, this should be your primary purpose as well.

Similarly, the activity leader must *value and respect people.* Every person is of value. We may look different, have different ages, interests, and abilities, but we are all worthy of being treated with dignity and respect. As an activity leader, you should exhibit this, and encourage this respect of others in your programs. Words as well as actions should build up one another, not tear them down.

The effective activity leader is *well-prepared.* She has materials ready, and a plan in place. As soon as the first participant arrives, she is ready to greet them and get them involved. Adequate preparation gives the leader confidence to interact with participants, to explain the events smoothly, and to enjoy the program along with the group.

The effective activity leader is *group-minded.* Even though he is the leader, he considers himself a part of the group. In referring to himself and the group, the effective activity leader says, “We.” While the ultimate responsibility for the group’s safety and enjoyment lies with the leader, he is willing to allow the group to make decisions and express their wishes.

The effective activity leader has some key personal qualities. She is *enthusiastic*, and demonstrates it through her voice and her actions. She is *humble*. When a game is not going well, she is not afraid to admit it and try something else. She is *creative*, both in selecting and presenting activities, as well as in maintaining group interest and control of the group. She exhibits a strong *sense of responsibility* for the group’s physical and emotional well-being. The effective activity leader has a *vision* for each person in the group: to help them grow and learn as a result of having been in the group.

It should be your goal as an activity leader to have each participant (and leader!) leave our program feeling better about themselves, and more a part of the group, than when they arrived. A lofty goal perhaps, but an attainable one with the right program and proper preparation. Chapter 2 will discuss some of the particulars in setting up and running your program.

CHAPTER 2

Planning For Your Group

So much of the success of your program results from the time you invest in its planning. Since every group and every leader is different, a number of factors need to be taken into consideration to help you decide what is "right" for each situation. We will look at them in this chapter.

Safety

Any game in which people are likely to get hurt is not a right choice. Certainly in many games there is a possibility of some injury. As an activity leader, you should take every precaution to assure your participants' safety. (Your participants—and/or their parents—will assume that you have.) Some suggestions:

1. Make sure you have played (or at least watched) every game you are going to lead. This will give you a better understanding of the game and its potential dangers, enabling you to modify or clarify the rules for safety depending upon the age or special needs of participants.

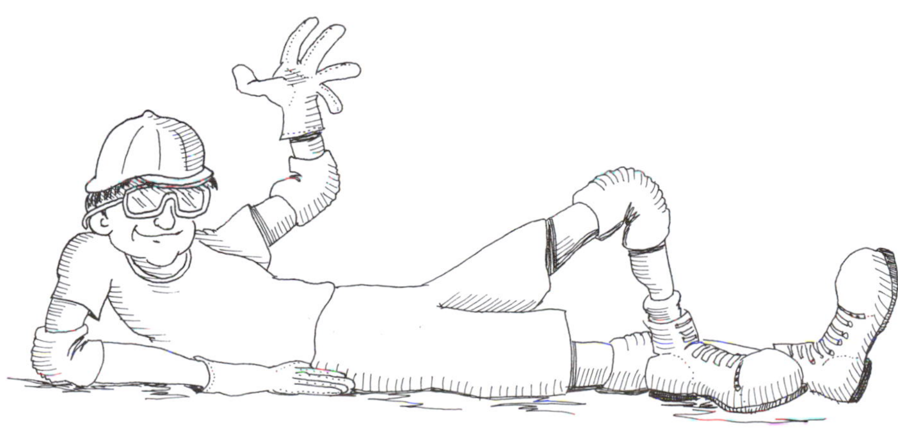

2. Examine the play area for any potential hazards before the first participant arrives. Eliminate hazards wherever possible. Mop up wet floors, remove or adequately pad protruding objects or obstacles, and so forth.

3. Warn (and later remind) participants of hazards they may encounter. Did you ever see a kid run out into the street after a ball? It is a classic illustration of how forgetful we can be of danger when we're distracted by fun.

4. If you are going to change or adapt a game, be sure to think through what the safety implications of those changes might be. Test the game out on some friends or co-workers, when possible.

5. Do *not* encourage participants to play roughly. It is easier to maintain safety in a group by establishing an atmosphere of fun and friendly competition than it is to try to calm down a bunch of wild and frenzied players. There is a difference between playing hard and playing roughly. Explain that to your group to minimize problems.

6. For physical, hard-hitting games, separate the sexes. Both sexes may enjoy the game, but it might be safer not to play co-ed.

7. Athletes will be athletes! "Competition" or "Dominance" may be their middle names. Encourage them to be team players. You might also give them a "handicap" for the game, such as hopping on one foot, or using their less dominant hand.

8. Be extra cautious in mixed groups that involve young children or older adults. It is easy for active, able-bodied people to assume everyone else is as hardy and as capable as they are. As the leader, you need to make sure the rules of the games you select are appropriate for your group, and that they assure the safety of your players. Make sure everyone is adhering to those rules.

9. Have first aid equipment on hand or readily available. The time to find out what to do in case of an emergency is *before* an emergency arises! Should an accident occur, you need to know where and how to get help.

10. Check your agency's accident policies to see what your responsibilities are in an emergency. Also check their **insurance coverage** to make sure all injuries will be adequately covered.

11. It is a good idea to require parental (or participant) release forms so immediate care can be given if anyone is injured.

Size of the Group

Some activities are great for small groups, but boring or disastrous for large groups. Conversely, large group games just don't play as well with only a few players. To assure maximum enjoyment for your group, select games appropriate for the number of participants you have.

Be prepared with alternatives or adaptations in case the number of people who show up for your program is drastically different from what you expected. Relays and tag games, for instance, are easily adaptable to a variety of group sizes. To be safe, though, have a few activity alternatives or variations up your sleeve (or jotted down on the back of a note card), just in case.

Age and Abilities of the Group

Knowing the ages and abilities of your group is also important for selecting appropriate activities. With children, a few years difference in age will make a tremendous difference in the skill level, interests, and social abilities of the participants. Select activities that are equally applicable to all age groups present, or consider dividing the group by age for specific activities.

If your group includes people of varied abilities, you may want to lead activities that focus more on cooperation than on competition. Team builders (see Chapter 5) require everyone's participation to successfully complete a task. Every person then feels that she has contributed to the game.

Another programming idea would be to chose "equalizer games." These are "nonskill" games, in which everyone is equally skilled (or unskilled). An example would be *Coin Toss* or *Lumberjack Contest.* A lot of fun can be had without a lot of athletic prowess. Simply stated, take into account the abilities of your group when planning for them.

Personality

Each group has its own unique personality. Some may be outgoing and gregarious, while others may be more reserved or "sophisticated." Don't be afraid to give the group new experiences, but do start off with activities that make the group feel comfortable. When people feel comfortable in a group, they are more likely to participate in unfamiliar activities. Establish a trusting atmosphere which will allow them to open up to the rest of the group. Keep in mind that some adults and children have been conditioned to be distrustful of new people and new things. Encourage them to participate without forcing them. They may warm up in time, and choose to join in when they are ready—especially if they see that you are having fun in an emotionally safe atmosphere.

Guard against choosing games solely on the basis of *your* enjoyment of them. Consider the personality of your group, and chose games that *they* would enjoy. They'll thank you for it, and your job will be easier and more enjoyable.

Purpose

The primary purposes of the games in this book are to promote positive self-esteem, to build a sense of community within your group, and of course, to have fun! Beyond that, you may have some underlying purposes: to have kids blow off some steam after a full day at school; to help your participants get to know each other better; to give people good, healthy exercise; or as a part of some special program. Whatever the purpose, you can orchestrate your program to be fun, and to accomplish these goals as well.

Ordering Your Activities

One key to a smoothly flowing program is the way in which you order your activities. Visualize your program as a wave. Start out gently, build up to a crest, then roll into a calming close. Begin your program before everyone arrives, with a *Group Starter* activity. This gets people involved in your program the minute they arrive, minimizing the "Well, now that I'm here, what do I do?" jitters.

Once everyone arrives, do some *Mixers* to get the whole group interacting with one other, and involved in your program. These can be simple games which require minimal instructions. Introductions to the people and the theme should be done at this point, if you haven't done so already.

What you fill the swell of the programming wave with is up to you. *Team Builders, Relays,* or *Active Games* all work well. For continuity sake, play several games in one formation before moving on to another. For example, playing several relays at once and then a circle game flows better

than doing one relay, a circle game, another relay, a tag game, then back to relay formation. Similarly, you may want to group activities which require the same "prop" together. Do several games with a Hula-Hoop,™ and then move on to games with other props.

Build excitement in your program to the *climax* activity: the curl of your programming wave. This climax activity might be *Kickball for All,* or the hilarious *Ridiculous Request Relay.* It is the highlight event of your program, and a memorable event. (Keep the camera handy!)

Alas! The fun can't go on forever, and the wave must break and gently wash away. To keep your participants from feeling like they've been body slammed down to the sand, do a *closing* activity or two. Select a *Quiet Game* or *Affirmation Activity* as a means of putting closure on a wonderful time together. Remember to thank each person for coming and being a part of the group. And encourage them to join you again!

Themes

Any time your group gets together to play some games can be fun. But when your program has a theme, you've got a party!

Whether it is a holiday season, or you just want it to feel like one, theme days can make for memorable programs. Creativity is the key for selecting a theme and for choosing accompanying activities. Give your group opportunities to contribute ideas. Sometimes the most far-fetched ideas can be formulated into the most creative and enjoyable of programs. Decorations, even minimal ones, can help set the appropriate mood. Modify activities to fit your theme. By changing the name or the prop used, you can adapt a game easily to your theme. A little background music, and theme-appropriate attire can also help reinforce your theme with the group. And if you are going to have refreshments, be sure to select something that ties in.

One More Thing

Please keep in mind that recreation activity planning is not a mathematical formula. These guidelines can't guarantee a perfect program, but they should help you as you plan. Review these guidelines, adopting what is appropriate for your particular situation. You, the leader, must be the judge of what is best for your group and for your program.

Remember, you are working with *people*, not numbers (well, at least not for this part of your job). As an activity leader, you need to be sensitive to your group, and figure out what works best for them. Plan a program of activities that you think will work for your group. Discuss your plans with your assistants or other staff members who may be familiar with your group. Be sure to have alternatives ready if what you have planned doesn't work.

After each program session, sit down and evaluate how it went. Note which activities or types of activities went well, and which ones bombed. While it's fresh in your mind, jot down ideas you have for organizing future groups or games, things to remember for next time, or any new ideas you might like to try in the future.

Think of your leadership abilities as muscles. The more you use them, the stronger they become. Just like getting into top physical shape, becoming a confident, skilled activity leader takes time and practice. There's no better time to begin your training than right now!

CHAPTER 3

Leading Your Group

In the last chapter, we talked about preparing for your group. Now we will look at the important task of preparing you, the leader. Effective group leadership begins before your group arrives, and continues after they have gone home. As the leader, you set the tone of the program. These hints will help you set a tone of enjoyment and acceptance, while maintaining control of your group.

Before You Begin

1. Make sure you have played the games you are going to lead. Having experienced the game firsthand, you will be more confident and competent at explaining the game, and at facilitating safe and fair play throughout.

2. Decide exactly what the rules will be before you stand up in front of the group. Practice giving the directions to your roommates, family, or other staff members. This practice will help increase your confidence when you are standing in front of your clientele.

3. Have some variations in mind to accommodate the group. What if only half of your group shows up? Or twice your normal crowd? What if the game is just too strenuous for their abilities? Be prepared with backup plans. You may not be prepared for everything that happens, but at least you will be prepared to do *something*.

4. Assemble all necessary equipment or props before the group arrives. Since flow of activities is important to maintaining interest and control of a group, the investment of time you make setting up will pay big dividends during your program. You'll have *continuity* between activities instead of *chaos*.

5. Visualize the whole program including the formations, props, and required energy levels of each game. Adjust the order of events for better flow of activities. This would include grouping games of similar formation together, or games using the same props together. (See Ordering Your Activities, in Chapter 2.)

6. If you have help, give a written plan of your order of activities to your assistant(s). This will allow them to prepare props, boundaries, and equipment for the next game, while you lead the current one. You must also decide on what leadership roles each will have for each game, or how they can best facilitate the fun and safety throughout the program.

7. Meet with the activities leadership team to review what you have planned, to clarify any questions or directions, to get any suggestions, and to remind each other that the participants and you are here to have fun!

In Front of the Group

1. Remember: enthusiasm is contagious! Your participants need to catch it from *you.* Your tone of voice and mannerisms convey your attitude about the program more convincingly than any words. If you have a great program planned, don't be shy about looking and sounding enthusiastic. Your enthusiasm will encourage others to participate, and will set them up for a fun time.

2. Get the group's attention before you begin speaking. Use a raised hand, a whistle, or hand clapping to draw the group around you. It is helpful to have a set policy, such as "when the hand goes up, the mouth goes shut." Giving a leader full (and quiet) attention is a learned skill. Once your group has learned it, you will find leading activities will go more smoothly and enjoyably.

3. Assemble your group in the formation required for the game before giving directions. (An exception to this would be a baseball type game, where players are spread out over a great distance.) Having players in close for the directions will save your throat, and keep the group's attention focused on you. Participants are also able to hear the instructions more clearly.

4. The formation of the game will dictate where you should be standing to give directions. Relay style formation, with players standing single file in teams, is a common formation for games in this book. Ask the teams to stand at an angle, or to sit while you demonstrate. This will enable them to see and hear better. For games in a circle formation, stand beside the players, as a group member, while you give directions. If it is necessary for you to stand in the center of the circle, be sure to turn so everyone can hear you.

5. If you are using a theme for the day, announce it at the beginning of your time together. Refer back to the theme as you move through your program, making tie-ins where possible.

6. Use brief anecdotes or stories to introduce activities. This adds interest, and sets the tone for the game.

7. Give clear, concise directions.

8. Demonstrate the activity. After you give the directions, demonstrate how to do it. Using assistants or yourself, run through the procedures to allow your participants to see what they are to do. Demonstrate and explain the "legal" ways of performing prescribed tasks.

9. A "dry run" of the game will often eliminate many of the questions people have about more complicated games. (And it will get them involved sooner.) Be sure to answer any questions that arise, or modify the rules if it appears to be necessary.

10. Encourage everyone to participate, but don't force them. Some people may feel physically unable to participate, or psychologically unprepared to join in. Respect a person's right to decline participation. Once the game is underway, you may want to check back with that person, to see if she might now feel more comfortable joining in. Or perhaps you might be able to use her as a referee, or in some other capacity.

11. Remember to encourage participants to play safely: both physically and emotionally. Bruised feelings often take longer to heal than bruised bodies. Let's do our best to prevent injuries of any type by reinforcing safety awareness.

As You Play

1. Maintain safety in the group. Stop play, whenever necessary, to modify the game to keep it safe. Remind players to play safely and courteously.

2. Be sensitive to how the game is going. Adjust the game as necessary to keep it fun and interesting, or to even out the teams. Don't be shy about calling a "time out" to modify the game when it's not going well. Chances are good your participants were hoping you would!

3. Encourage players verbally. Let them know you value their *efforts*, not just their *performance*.

4. Nip cheating in the bud! The spirit of play is joyful, even in competition. When someone, or some team, does not play fairly, the joyful spirit of play is broken, and everyone loses.

5. Be alert for the best time to select a new "It" or a new game. This will help keep things flowing, and everyone enthusiastic (especially the person who had been "It" too long!).

6. Participate in the game yourself. Unless it is necessary for you to referee, or facilitate the play in some other way, join in the game too. This will help you keep a finger on the pulse of the game, as well has help you build rapport with the participants.

7. It is better to end a game while it is going strong, than to play it so long that it "dies." If it was healthy when you quit playing the game, the game will likely be well-received the next time you suggest playing it.

8. Allow your participants the opportunity to provide some input into activity selection. They may know a fun variation to the game you are playing, or may have a suggestion for a different activity. Be flexible in accommodating their ideas, while remembering that *you* are still ultimately responsible for the group's safety and enjoyment.

Ideas for Choosing Teams

Since our goal is "play to have fun," selecting teams should be fun, too. Having captains pick teams is usually *not* fun, especially if you are one of the last ones picked. To remedy this, here are some suggestions for less intimidating ways of choosing teams:

- Line up your group tallest to shortest. Then count off by the number of teams you want to have (1, 2, 3, 1, 2, 3. . .).
- Line up the group guy/gal/guy/gal. Have the group count off by fours. The 1's and 2's become one team, and the 3's and 4's another.
- Divide up the group according to birth months (January, February, and March together; April, May, and June; and so on.).
- Try breaking them up according to the seasons in which they were born.
- Ask your players to form three groups based on day of the month they were born (1st -10th, group 1; 11th -20th, group 2; 21st -31st, group 3).
- Group them according to the color of shirts/clothes.
- Draw groups from a hat. Have slips of paper in the hat that will distinguish different teams by:
    - Colors
    - Animal names (they must find their group by making the animals' sounds)
    - Simple, familiar song titles (they must find their group by singing or humming their song)

- Frames of comic strips from Sunday's paper. Each person draws a frame, then must find her group, and assemble the strip in chronological order.
- Names of different types of ethnic foods. One team might be all Mexican food, another Chinese, and a third might look like a McDonald's menu.

You might want to "randomly" divide the team yourself, by handing out team indicators yourself. This would allow you to even out the teams in terms of physical ability or some other characteristic. Team indicators could include:

- Different flavored pieces of gum.
- Candy pieces wrapped in different colored foil.
- Balloons of as many different colors as you want teams.
- Theme-related name tags or pictures.
- Strips of flagging tape or ribbon to use as headbands or armbands.

Dividing Your Group in Half

Dividing your group into teams using a random number generator might be an interesting study in probability theory, but why not try one of these more interesting suggestions for splitting your group in two?

- *Odd or Even.* On the count of three, have each player throw out one or two fingers—no changing them once they're out! Make one team the evens, the other team is, well, odd.
- *Second Letter Split.* All those players who have a vowel for the second letter of their first name move to one side of the line. Those with consonant second letters move to the other side.
- *Flip a Coin.* What could be more fair? Heads, one team; tails, the other.
- *Observation Designation.* Look your group over. What do you see as an obvious way to break into two groups? Shorts vs. long pants. Short hair vs. long hair. (You may have to explain what you consider long for the guys and for the gals.) Sneakers vs. street shoes. T-shirts vs. others. Look at your people. It may be obvious, and can be fun!

Ways to Select "IT"

"One, two, three—Not It!" That's how we always did it as kids—and somehow, I always ended up being It (regardless of when I yelled, "Not It"). So, if you are looking for a more enjoyable (and fair!) way of selecting an "It," try one of these:

- *Number "It."* Someone calls out a number appreciably larger than the number of players. Have the group line up and count off until you get to the given number. That person is "It."
- *One, two, three, Shoot!* Similar to "Number It." To determine what the large number will be, players hold out one, two, or three fingers on the command "Shoot." Total the number of fingers, and count out that many places to "It." (Say, wouldn't that be an interesting way to divide the group into three teams?)
- *Alphabet "It."* Each person says a letter of the alphabet, in order. If you say the first letter of your first or last name, you get to sit down. The last one standing is "It."

Keeping Score

Keeping track of team points can add excitement to a special program, such as *Lumberjack Daze,* or *Relay Day.* Do you want to make it really exciting? Be really extravagant with your point giving. Since it doesn't cost you any more, why not make a first place finish worth 1000 points? Second could be worth 800, third, 600, and fourth, 400. Talk about motivation! You'll have kids flocking to your program, because they would rather play for a thousand points than for five. Or maybe you would rather consider yourself a multi-millionaire. Give away fabulous (play) money prizes. "The jackpot for this next event is $10,000!" There's no telling *who* might join in the fun with this kind of score keeping!

CHAPTER 4

Group Starters And Mixers

Remember walking into class the first day of school? Remember how awkward you felt? Remember how you didn't know anyone, and how you wondered if you ever would? Well, if you want to help minimize the anxiety, and maximize the enjoyment for your participants, here's the chapter for you.

Group Starters are activities that are designed to get people involved with your program from the minute they step through the door. By giving your participants something fun to do as they arrive, you can help them become more at ease, and more ready to join in with the rest of your program. These activities can be individually oriented, such as "guess the number of jelly beans in a jar," or something that involves interacting with others, as in *Duel.*

Regardless of the activity you choose as a Group Starter, please do take a minute with each participant as he or she comes in. Personally welcome them. Let them know you are glad that they came to join in the fun, and that they *can* expect to have a fun time here!

Take advantage of this personal welcoming time to begin establishing a trusting, caring atmosphere in your program. Find out your participants' names and tell them yours. Use their names when addressing them, and introduce them to others. Because of this effort on your part, participants will respond enthusiastically to your program. More importantly, they will likely be uplifted and encouraged as a person. And that is, after all, the ultimate goal of our recreation programs.

Review the activities suggested here, and give them a try. See what kind of props you have readily available, and modify the games accordingly. These types of activities can be readily adapted to your theme. For *Beach Day,* for example, guess the number of shells in the jar, or try to unscramble a list of "scrambled" beach-related words. Group Starters are an excellent way to introduce your theme. So remember, even before everyone has assembled, you can begin the fun.

The following activities are broken down into two sections: group starters and mixers. Both types of activities warm the group up to your program. The basic difference is that group starters are used with individuals as they arrive, and mixers are initiated when the whole group has assembled. Group Starters and Mixers are sort of the "one-two" punch for getting your program off to a great start!

Caption Writing Contest

Place	Indoors
Players	Any Number
Time	As Available
Energy	Minimal

Here's a chance to bring out the comic in each of us. Post a humorous picture, and have everyone caption it. You'll be amazed at the quick wit of your group!

EQUIPMENT

- One or more cartoons or pictures to be captioned
- Paper and pencils
- Box for submitting captions

PREPARATION

Post the pictures on the wall, with an entry box located beneath.

TO PLAY

As participants arrive, hand them paper and pencils, and ask them to write a caption for each picture. Have them put their names on the back of their entry. When all entries are submitted, have a panel of judges select the best one. Or post all entries, and let the participants vote on their favorites.

Face Up Card Toss

Place	Indoors
Players	Any Number
Time	As Available
Energy	Minimal

Here's a challenging stunt that is so simple, people will want to give it another try, and another, and another! Set it up before your group arrives for individual play, or have groups sign up for team competitions.

EQUIPMENT

- One deck of playing cards
- An empty, large coffee can, or wash and dry the bottom half of a gallon milk jug
- Masking tape to mark throwing line

FORMATION

Players line up behind the throwing line to take a turn. The can/jug should be placed approximately 3 to 4 feet away.

TO PLAY

In turn, each player is given one suit of a deck of cards (13 cards in all). She then pitches them one at a time, trying to get them to land inside the jug. Once all the cards have been pitched, the player tallies her score. Each card that lands in the jug is worth twice its face value. For instance, if a "7" went in, it would be worth 14 points. Cards that land face up on the floor around the jug are worth face value toward the score. The Jack, Queen, and King are each worth 12 points, and the Ace is worth 15 points in this game. Cards that land face down on the floor are worth zero points. Gather up the cards, and see if you can score higher next time!

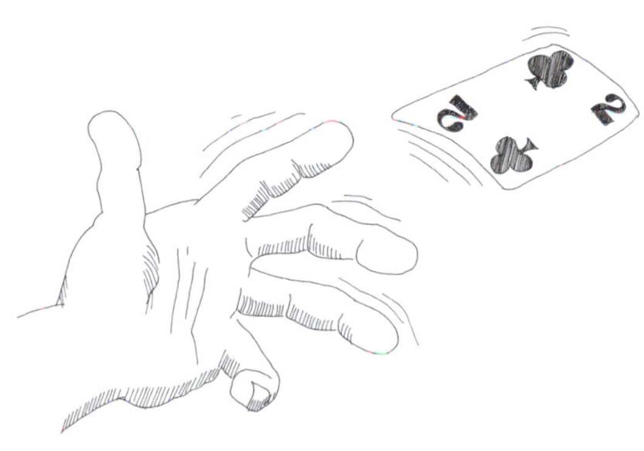

The Nose Knows

Place	Indoors
Players	Any Number
Time	As Available
Energy	Minimal

Set these jars out and see how well your group does at identifying common scents.

EQUIPMENT

- A dozen or so jars with lids (reclosable plastic bags and empty film canisters work well, too)
- Cotton balls
- A variety of extracts or odorous substances, such as vanilla or almond extract, finely grated lemon or orange peel, vinegar, perfume. (Please *avoid* using chemicals which warn: DO NOT INHALE!)
- Pencils and paper for each participant

PREPARATION

With liquid aromas, sprinkle a few drops of the substance on a cotton ball, and place in a covered jar. For solid substances, such as grated lemon peel, or chocolate chips, conceal them in an unscented tissue before placing them in the jar. Prepare the jars a day in advance, to allow the aroma to permeate the tissue and the jar. Label each jar numerically, and make a master answer sheet with the correct identities.

TO PLAY

Each participant opens a jar, and sniffs the contents, trying to determine its identity. When he thinks he knows what it is, the player jots down the number of the jar and his guess on his sheet of paper. After he has sniffed all the scents, he compares his guesses with the answer sheet. (He will inevitably go back to smell again the ones he identified incorrectly!)

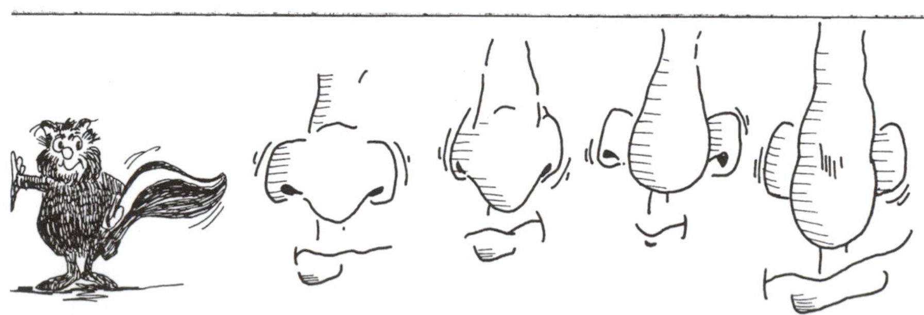

Place	Indoors/Outdoors
Players	Any Number
Time	As Available
Energy	Minimal

Taste Testers

At Penn State, where I went to college, the Food Science Department sometimes held taste testing experiments. They needed students to survey, and I always enjoyed getting a free ice cream cone for participating in one of their studies. It was a great, albeit infrequent, relationship! Anyway, you can set up your own "scientific study" for your group to enjoy.

EQUIPMENT

- 3-ounce paper cups, sufficient for each participant to have one for each liquid to be tasted
- 5-ounce paper cups (same number as above, to act as lids)
- Toothpicks, or other pointed object to pierce hole in the bottom of the 5-ounce cups, to allow the straw to slip in
- Cocktail sipping straws, or standard straws, cut into 2 shorter straws
- A variety of liquids to sample and identify
- Pencils and paper for each player

PREPARATION

Before your group arrives, fill (half way) the 3-ounce cups with several different liquids. Pierce the bottom of a 5-ounce cup, and invert it over the filled cup. Insert a straw in the hole. Group the cups on a table, with alphabetical labels for each group.

TO PLAY

As your participants arrive, give each one a pencil and sheet of paper. Have them take a cup from group A, taste it, and try to identify it. Have them mark their guess on the paper next to the letter A. Ask them to repeat this process for each of the other taste-test items.

You may choose liquids of similar taste to sample, such as cranberry juice vs. cranapple juice, or Coke® vs. Pepsi.® Or you might want to set up the activity for taste preference. Do you prefer the taste of "A" or "B"? (Wouldn't you love to find out your group actually *preferred* the store brand soda to the name brand stuff!)

Come to think of it, there's no need to limit taste testing to liquids. Set up taste preference tests for your group with foods, too. Compare generic potato chips to name brands, Hershey's® chocolate chips to Nestlé®, or store brand cereals to the fancy boxed ones. Place a small amount of the test food in a 3-ounce cup labeled "A" or "B," and let your group cast their votes. "And the winner of the best tasting nacho-flavored tortilla chip is..."

Place	Indoors/Outdoors
Players	Any Number
Time	As Available
Energy	Minimal

Nature I.D.

You don't have to be a licensed naturalist to enjoy the incredible diversity and intricacy of our natural world. Nature I.D. is a great way to introduce a nature-related program, or simply to encourage your group to appreciate the wonders of nature.

EQUIPMENT

- A dozen or more specimens from nature
- Pencils and paper for each player
- Answer sheet, or nature guide books to allow players to research for themselves what the items are

PREPARATION

Before your group arrives, lay out the articles on a table, labeled "A," "B," "C," and so on. Consider using specimens of leaves, bark, shells, or wildflowers.

TO PLAY

As participants arrive, hand them each a paper and pencil, and challenge them to identify the different items from nature. If desired, set out nature guide books for them to use to help them with their identifications. See how well people are able to identify the items, and spend a few minutes providing the group with interesting information about each.

Seed I.D.

Place	Indoors/Outdoors
Players	Any Number
Time	As Available
Energy	Minimal

Gardeners and nongardeners alike will enjoy the challenge of identifying different seeds—and be quite enlightened!

EQUIPMENT

- A dozen or more varieties of seeds
- Material to mount them: either clear packing tape to seal around each variety, or cardboard and glue to make display cards. (Label each card A, B, C, and so on, and have a master sheet with key)
- Pencil and paper for each participant

TO PLAY

Lay out seed cards. Allow participants to examine the cards, and make their best guess at what type of seed each is. After everyone has had an opportunity to write them down, give the identification of each seed. The responses may be quite surprising!

Place	Indoors
Players	Any Number
Time	As Available
Energy	Minimal

Bubble Blowing Contest

So you think your group is full of hot air? Great! They need to be for this game!

EQUIPMENT

- Jar(s) of bubble soap with wand
- Hula-Hoop™ or other large ring
- String
- Masking tape and pen

PREPARATION

Suspend the Hula-Hoop™ from the ceiling with the string, so the bottom of the hoop is at chest height for your average participant.

TO PLAY

Using the wand to blow bubbles, players take turns seeing how far from the hoop they can stand, and still blow bubbles through the Hula-Hoop™ opening. Mark each person's best effort on the floor with a piece of masking tape. Label the tape with the contestant's name. The person with the most hot air (furthest distance from the hoop) wins a bottle of bubble soap!

Scrambled Valentines

Place	Indoors
Players	Any Number
Time	5 Minutes
Energy	Minimal

Unscrambling words can be a great group starter for any program. Just change the words to match your theme!

EQUIPMENT

- Pencil and prepared sheet for each player

TO PLAY

Each participant tries to unscramble these Valentine's Day (or other theme) related words.

1. AYDNC (CANDY)
2. ORLVE (LOVER)
3. EVLNNTAIE (VALENTINE)
4. SOSRE (ROSES)
5. WORSELF (FLOWERS)
6. TTEHWEASRE (SWEETHEART)
7. STARHE (HEARTS)
8. PCDUI (CUPID)
9. SATCCOEOLH (CHOCOLATES)
10. ARMNOCE (ROMANCE)

Coin Toss

Place	Indoors
Players	Any Number
Time	As Available
Energy	Minimal

A great equalizer game. Sounds so simple, yet you'll want to try "just once more!"

EQUIPMENT

- Large glass fish bowl or mixing bowl full of water
- Small glass cup
- Several coins

PREPARATION

Set the small glass cup on the bottom of the large glass bowl. Set the large bowl on a low table, and fill it with water.

TO PLAY

Hand the first contestant a few coins, and challenge them to drop them into the small cup, which is inside the larger bowl. It's not as easy as it seems, as the water makes it do funny things.

Duel

Place	Indoors/Outdoors
Players	2 or More
Time	As Available
Energy	Moderate

The invention of washable markers has revolutionized this game. Mom doesn't yell like she used to when we dueled with permanent markers as kids!

EQUIPMENT

- A washable marker per player
- An old extra-large shirt or smock per player, if desired. (Boys may want to play with no shirt on)
- Stopwatch or watch with second hand

FORMATION

This game requires play to be in pairs, standing in an area of approximately 10 feet in diameter.

TO PLAY

Hand both players a marker. On "Go," the players remove the cap, keeping it in their weaker hand, which they hold behind their back. With the marker in their dominant hand, players try to mark up their opponents torso as much as possible. Arms, chest, belly, and back are all fair targets. At the end of 60 seconds, players recap their markers, and get a good look at themselves. The player with the least amount of marker on them is the winner. Wash off the marker, and find a new partner!

Penny Pondering

Place	Indoors
Players	Any Number
Time	5 Minutes
Energy	Minimal

No longer will you take a mere penny for granted! There's a lot to a penny when you stop to examine it!

EQUIPMENT

- Prepared question sheet and pencil for each participant
- Penny for each participant

TO PLAY

As participants arrive, hand each one a pencil, a penny, and the prepared question sheet.

On a Lincoln head penny locate the following:

1. A serving of corn *(ear)*
2. A fruit *(date)*
3. A type of flower *(two lips)*
4. A type of hot or cold beverage *("T" or tea)*
5. Large body of salt water *("C" or sea)*
6. A rabbit *(hair)*
7. Part of a needle *(eye)*
8. Part of a stream, as it enters a river *(mouth)*
9. A messenger is . . . *(one cent, or one sent)*
10. A sacred place *(temple)*
11. Wooden part of railroad tracks *(tie)*
12. The side of a road *(shoulder)*

Pin A Pal

Place	Indoors
Players	Pairs
Time	As Available
Energy	Moderate

Here's a frantic game—even with players seated in chairs!

EQUIPMENT

- Two chairs
- Twenty clothespins plus extras
- Two blindfolds
- Stopwatch or watch with second hand

TO PLAY

Have 2 players sit face-to-face in the two chairs, with their knees nearly touching. Give each player 10 clothespins, and blindfold each. On the "Go!" command, players have 60 seconds to pin as many clothespins on each other as possible. They may remove clothespins from themselves to place on their opponent, or retrieve them from the floor, if possible. At the end of one minute, call time, remove the blindfolds, and see which player has the fewest pins.

As supplies, people, and enthusiasm allows, you may want to set this game up as a round robin tournament. Or, have players line up in two rows of chairs for team action!

Mixers

Now that your participants have been warmed up with Group Starters, it is time to move on to Mixers. These activities are designed to help your group members get to know one another, and to begin interacting in a nonthreatening way. Whether your group is getting together for the first time, or on a regular basis, Mixers get your program moving.

Name Toss

Place	Indoors/Outdoors
Players	8 to 20
Time	5 Minutes
Energy	Minimal

Names. We've all got one. They are a part of who we are. By getting to know someone's name, you tell that person you care about them. Even if you have to ask me my name a dozen times, I'm glad you care enough to want to know it! Here's a simple game to help your group get to know one another's names.

EQUIPMENT

- One tennis-type ball, (or more, optional)

FORMATION

Have the group and leaders stand in a circle, about arm's-length apart, facing center.

TO PLAY

The leader starts with the ball, states her name, then tosses the ball to the person to her left (or right). That person says his name, and continues the ball along its way around the circle. Each person in turn says her name, until the ball returns to the leader. Hopefully, everyone has remembered at least one other person's name. If not, pass the ball around again!

The game really gets rolling when the leader calls the name of someone in the circle, and lofts the ball to him. That person catches it, calls out someone else's name, and tosses the ball on to her. On the game goes, with group members learning each others' names as they go!

VARIATIONS

After the group has tossed names around for a few minutes, add a second ball to the action. If your group is up to the challenge (or simply enjoys the chaos), add even more balls!

If your group is so large you have to divide it into several circles, ask several people from each group to move to another circle. This will help everyone get to know more people. Be sure you review names every time someone new joins your group.

Pet Peeve Pass

Place	Indoors/Outdoors
Players	10 to 30
Time	5 Minutes
Energy	Minimal

A group of students led this game at the end of a semester together. It proved to be quite enlightening for all of us!

EQUIPMENT

- A tennis ball or foam ball

FORMATION

Have your group sit in a tight circle.

TO PLAY

In turn, a player says his name, then shares with the group one of his pet peeves: that is, something that really bothers him. It is amazing how many frustrations we have in common, from missing a parking meter "feeding," to choosing the "wrong" line to wait in, or having the power go out when you are about to set a new world record on a video game!

Human Twister

Place	Indoors
Players	15 to 30
Time	5 Minutes
Energy	Minimal

This game was a spontaneous creation by a couple of fun-loving students in response to the directive: here are some everyday supplies, make up something fun to do with them. This is the ditty they came up with. We enjoyed getting tangled up in it, and I think you will, too!

EQUIPMENT

- Colored slips of paper (3 x 5 card size)
- Masking tape

PREPARATION

Before your group arrives, cut paper of 4 or 5 different colors into rectangles or shapes of approximately 3" x 5" size. You will need enough paper cards for each participant to receive two cards from the total number cut.

TO PLAY

As people arrive, give them each 2 different colored cards, and 2 strips of masking tape. Ask them to tape the cards to two places on their bodies. (For example, their left shoulder and their right knee.) When everyone has taped on the cards, challenge the group to line up, matching (and touching) their cards to someone else's of the same color.

The resulting effect may be quite humorous, as one person tries to link his left elbow with another persons right ankle, at the same time he's trying to press his right ear to a third person's left shoulder! Have the group maintain contact long enough for you to snap a picture of the twisted, tangled appendage pile. "Everyone smile!"

Place	Indoors/Outdoors
Players	10 to 35
Time	5 Minutes
Energy	Minimal

Group Juggling

Group juggling is not as strenuous or as dangerous as the title may lead you to believe! Actually, the balls are what get juggled, and the group cooperatively does the juggling. Now that that's cleared up, on with the game!

EQUIPMENT

- Several tennis balls

FORMATION

Ask the group to stand in a circle, arm's-length apart, with their own hands held together in front of them.

TO PLAY

The leader begins with a ball, calls someone's name, then tosses the ball to him. That person catches the ball, and then selects someone on the other side of the circle to toss it to. If he doesn't know her name, he may ask, of course, and then toss the ball on to her. Once he has tossed the ball onto someone, the thrower puts his hands behind his back. This lets other tossers know that he has already been part of the juggling sequence, and that they should select someone else to receive their lob. When everyone has received the ball from someone else, it is passed back to the leader. (**NOTE:** Each person needs to remember who tossed the ball to them, and to whom they passed to ball along to, as this sequence is what makes group juggling work!) The leader then reinitiates the group juggling sequence, and the same pattern of tosses continues. As the group becomes more confident in their ability to smoothly send the sphere about the circle, add a second ball. And a third. And a fourth!? Your group will be pleased (and maybe a little surprised!) at how well they can collectively keep these spheres aloft!

The Mystery Mingler

Place	Indoors/Outdoors
Players	20 or More
Time	5 Minutes
Energy	Minimal

This game is better than playing the lottery: the odds of winning are greater, and you get a chance to meet some new people!

EQUIPMENT

- Several small tokens per Mystery Mingler
- As many small "prizes" as you have tokens
- A prearranged "Mystery Mingler" or more, depending on the size of your group

PREPARATION

Estimate the number of participants, and the supply of small prizes you have available, such as lollipops, packs of gum, or new pencils. (With 20 people, you might have one Mystery Mingler pass out 5 tokens.) Before everyone arrives, select one person (or more, if your group will be large) to be the Mystery Mingler for this game. Slip him the small tokens, and in a hushed voice explain the details of their devious mission: they are to slip a token into the hand of every 10th person they shake hands with.

TO PLAY

With your group together en masse, explain that there is a Mysterious Mingler in their midst. This unknown celebrity is extremely eccentric, and generous. To meet this person, everyone must mingle around, shaking hands with everyone else, exchanging pleasantries and polite conversation. If anyone should find a small token in his hand, simply hold on to it, and continue along as if nothing had happened. Allow the group to begin their mingling. After several minutes of socializing, ask anyone who has a token to come forward. (If there are not as many people stepping forward as there were tokens to be given out, let the mingling continue.) Once all the tokens have been accounted for, reveal the Mystery Mingler to a round of enthusiastic applause! Then invite those holding tokens to exchange them for their prizes.

Place	Indoors/Outdoors
Players	12 to 24
Time	10 to 15 Minutes
Energy	Minimal

Allow Me To Introduce To You...

It is often a difficult thing to stand up in front of a group of people you barely know, and tell them about yourself. With this activity, you end up learning about one another, but by way of introduction.

EQUIPMENT

- None

TO PLAY

Ask your group members to pair up with someone they have just met, or someone that they do not know well. Have pairs position themselves around the room, so they can talk together comfortably. Each person is to find out a little about the other person, so they can introduce them to the rest of the group. Suggested topics of conversation could include: name, home town, year in school, hobbies, sports, favorite subjects, favorite animals, and the like. After giving each partner 3 to 4 minutes to talk, bring the group back together, and have them sit in a circle. In turn, each person stands and introduces their partner to the group.

This is an especially effective get-to-know-you activity for groups who will be meeting together repeatedly, such as classes or camps. It helps speed the process of finding people with similar interests within the group. Every person is unique and interesting. And after this activity, you'll have things to talk about with each other.

Getting-To-Know-You Backrubs

Place	Indoors/Outdoors
Players	Any Number
Time	20 to 30 Minutes
Energy	Minimal

Do you want a fun way to help your group get to know each other, and relieve some tension at the same time? Then this is the activity for you! Each person must give and receive backrubs to/from people who meet the criteria outlined on their form. (If only every *form we had to fill out was this enjoyable!)*

EQUIPMENT

- Prepared forms for each participant
- Pencil or pen for each player

TO PLAY

Hand out pencils and a copy of the prepared forms to each player. Tell your group they have 20 minutes to complete their form, and the following rules apply:

1. No one may *receive* two backrubs in a row.
2. You may not refuse to give or receive a backrub from anyone who asks you.
3. You must have the person who *gives* you a backrub, or who *receives* one from you, initial your form. No initial, no score.
4. The person who receives a backrub from you scores its quality on a scale of 1 (poor) to 10 (excellent), and marks this on your form next to her/his initials.
5. You score 5 points for every backrub you receive.
6. You may have the same person's initials on your form only twice: once to give a backrub, once to receive.
7. The person with the highest score at the end of the allotted time wins.

A SAMPLE BACKRUB FORM:

1. Give a backrub to someone who has never been outside of the U.S.
2. Receive a backrub from someone who has traveled outside the U.S.
3. Give a backrub to someone who has a birthday in a month with an "r" in it.
4. Receive a backrub from someone who has a birthday in a month with no "r" in it.
5. Give a backrub to someone who has flown on an airplane.
6. Receive a backrub from someone who has never flown on an airplane.
7. Give a backrub to someone who has never ridden on a train.
8. Receive a backrub from someone who has ridden on a train.
9. Give a backrub to someone who does not like cats.
10. Receive a backrub from someone who loves cats.
11. Give a backrub to someone who has a brother or sister.
12. Receive a backrub from someone who has no brothers or sisters.
13. Give a backrub to someone who has a vowel as the first letter of their first (or last) name.
14. Receive a backrub from someone whose first name begins with a consonant.
15. Give a backrub to someone who exercises regularly.
16. Receive a backrub from someone who enjoys watching a lot of television, or playing Nintendo.™
17. Give a backrub to someone who wears glasses or contact lenses.
18. Receive a backrub from someone who does not wear glasses or contact lenses.
19. Give a backrub to someone who can play a musical instrument.
20. Receive a backrub from someone who enjoys using computers.

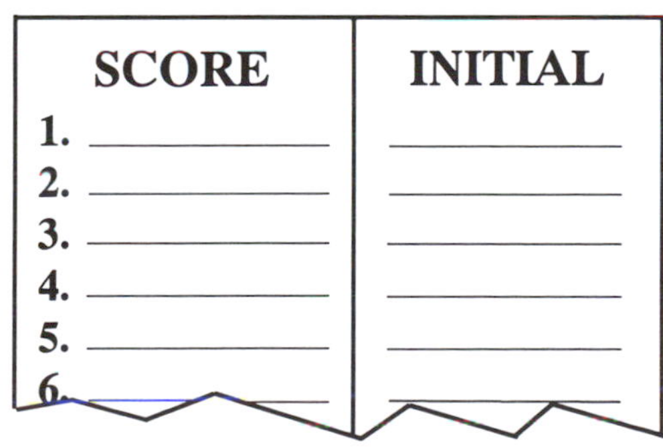

SCORE	INITIAL
1. ______	______
2. ______	______
3. ______	______
4. ______	______
5. ______	______
6. ______	______

I Say, It's A Beautiful Day!

Place	Indoors/Outdoors
Players	12 to 24
Time	5 Minutes
Energy	Minimal

EQUIPMENT

- None

FORMATION

Seat your group in a circle.

TO PLAY

The leader begins by turning to the person sitting next to her, and says loudly, "I, Annette, say, 'It's a beautiful day!'" That person then turns to the person on the other side of him, and says loudly enough for everyone to hear, "Annette told me, Roger, that 'It's a beautiful day!'" The message is passed around the circle, with each person adding his or her name to the list as it moves along. Since the objective of this game is to learn each other's names, it is OK to help a fellow player out by prompting her on a forgotten name. Once everyone has had a turn, you might want to challenge someone to give everyone's name. Then move on to another activity, and enjoy the beautiful day!

Place	Indoors/Outdoors
Players	12 to 24
Time	5 Minutes
Energy	Minimal

I'm Going To Montana

I've never been to Montana personally. My husband says he's going to take me there this summer. And when I go, I'm going to take with me . . .

EQUIPMENT

- None

FORMATION

Have your group sit or stand in a circle, so everyone can clearly see everyone else.

TO PLAY

Select a first person who begins by saying, "My name is Marinna. I'm going to Montana, and I'm taking a _____." Silently, she pantomimes something she might take along, such as a comb, toothbrush, camera, hat, Sony® Walkman™ or whatever comes to mind. The next person in the circle says, "My name is Joe, and I'm going to Montana with Marinna. We're going to take ___(what Marinna pantomimed), and _____ (something that Joe has thought of)." On along the circle it goes, until everyone has had a turn—and you start looking for a bus and trailer to make this trip to Montana a reality!

Laugh Pass (or What to Do After You Wipe That Silly Grin Off Your Face!)

Place	Indoors/Outdoors
Players	12 to 24
Time	5 Minutes
Energy	Minimal

Laughing can be so contagious. So self-control is the big challenge in this game, especially when you've got an really animated laugher taking a turn!

EQUIPMENT

- None

FORMATION

The group sits in a circle for this most solemn of games.

TO PLAY

The leader explains that he has something, like a new product or discovery, that will be passed or tossed around the circle. Everyone will get a turn to test it out. Those who are watching the experimenters must watch respectfully, keeping a straight face at all times. The leader then reaches into an imaginary bag or his pocket, and quickly pulls out and puts on a ridiculous and silly, laughing face. Only the person who "has" the laughing face may laugh. He may, however, take a few moments to explore the humorous possibilities this face affords. When he has finished, he wipes that silly grin off his face, and passes or tosses it to someone else in the circle. As the leader, keep the face (uh, pace) moving, making sure everyone gets a turn. Then return the laughing face to the "bag," only to discover there are enough of these for everyone! Quickly toss out laughing faces to everyone, and enjoy the crescendo of laughter!

Place	Indoors
Players	24 or More
Time	5 Minutes
Energy	Maximum

Newspaper Delivery

Talk about a good way to let out your emotions! Newspaper Delivery is a quick-burst of a group mixer!

EQUIPMENT

- Large stack of newspapers for each team
- Approximately 50 feet of rope

FORMATION

Divide your group in two. Place half of the group on each side of the rope, which has been strung across the middle of the playing area, at a height of 4 feet.

TO PLAY

Give each team a sizable stack of old newspapers. On "Go," team members begin crumpling up sheets of newspaper, and "deliver" them *over* the rope to the opposite team. Simultaneously, the opposing team is doing their best to "deliver" their newspapers, as well as returning any that may have been sent over by the other team.

After three or four minutes, call for a cease fire. The team with the least amount of crumpled up newspaper on their side is declared the winner. Follow up this game with a Paper Bag Stuff. See which team can stuff their newspaper wads into paper bags faster. Then recycle them!

Newspaper Puzzler

Place	Indoors
Players	18 to 30
Time	5 Minutes
Energy	Minimal

The key to making this game challenging is in the preparation on the paper puzzles. Cut out similarly sized shapes from each of the sheets of newspaper. Then players will have to scramble around more, trying to locate just the right one.

EQUIPMENT

- A sheet of newspaper for each team, from which shapes have been cut. Save the cutouts. Make 5 or 6 cutouts per page. Use similar designs for all the sheets. For example, cut out several stars, hearts, or snowflake designs from each sheet. (This is most easily done by making a fold in the paper, and cutting out as one would Valentine's hearts.) Make a few extra cutout pieces from other newspaper sheets.

FORMATION

Divide your group into teams of 5 or 6. Have them line up relay style. Scatter the cutouts from ALL of the newspapers (and a few extra cutouts) in an area approximately 30 feet from the starting line.

TO PLAY

Give one person from each team a sheet of newspaper with cutout holes. On "Go," other team members run up to the area where the cutouts are scattered. They may each bring back only one, which they hand to the holder of the newspaper. This person checks to see if the piece fits. If it does, great. If not, the person who brought it must take it back to the pile, and select another piece.

The first team to successfully complete their newspaper puzzle wins!

Place	Indoors/Outdoors
Players	Any Number
Time	5 Minutes
Energy	Minimal

"Do This" Mixer

Your group will get mingling on this one, for sure!

EQUIPMENT

- None

FORMATION

To begin, have your group stand in a circle. Once directions are given, they will scatter.

TO PLAY

Every person whispers to the person to her right a command, which they are to carry out with three different people. For example, a person may be requested to untie and retie three people's shoes, or propose to three different people, or sing them a song, give backrubs, or simply shake their hands and introduce themselves. A bit of bedlam to begin your program can be loads of fun!

Blown Up Blender

Place	Indoors
Players	16 or More
Time	5 Minutes
Energy	Moderate

To tailor this mixer to suit your group and your program, just write up messages that are appropriate for your purposes. Groups love to play this game: it combines the action of a relay with the suspense of a secret mission!

EQUIPMENT

- One inflated balloon per team, with "mission" slip inside

FORMATION

Divide your group into even relay teams of 8 to 10 players each. Have them line up relay style.

TO PLAY

Hand the first person in each team a specially prepared, inflated balloon. On "Go," the balloon gets passed "Under/Over" to the back of the line, and then back to the front of the line. When the balloon is returned to the first person in line, he sits on it to pop it. The note is retrieved, and passed to the last person in line, who reads it aloud. The entire team must then perform the prescribed task. The first team to successfully complete their task wins!

SUGGESTED TASKS:

- Without speaking, have your group line up according to month and day of birth (not year), with January at the front of the line, December at the end.
- Without speaking, line up your group alphabetically by first (or last) names, with A at the front, and Z at the back.
- Have your group stand with arms on one another's shoulders and sing "America, the Beautiful."
- Have your group use their bodies collectively to spell out the word "Hello."
- Have your group do 20 jumping jacks, counting LOUDLY!

Human Taco

Place	Indoors
Players	18 or More
Time	5 Minutes
Energy	Moderate

Human Tacos: a sort of tag, with a Mexican flavor!

EQUIPMENT

- Adhesive tags, or note cards and tape, labeled with taco ingredients

FORMATION

Scattered.

TO PLAY

As each person arrives, stick a label on the back of their shirt. Then they mingle around asking "Yes/No" questions to determine which taco ingredient they are. Once everyone has ascertained whether they're a Taco Shell, Meat, Cheese, Lettuce, Tomato, or Salsa, the action begins!

Explain the "proper" order in assembling a taco, as described below. On the "I'm Hungry! Let's Eat!" command, the Taco Shells begin searching for the next logical ingredient: the Meat. When a Taco Shell locates a Meat, she grabs his hand, and the two go darting off to locate a Cheese. Then the three race around to find a Lettuce, then Tomato, then Salsa, in that order. Players, of course, can try to conceal their ingredient tag, by moving evasively. The first taco completely built wins a box of Hot Tamales™ (candy)!

Pick A Partner

Place	Indoors
Players	12 to 40
Time	5 Minutes
Energy	Minimal

Pick a Partner is most effectively played with a group that knows one another fairly well. And it's interesting to see what people learn and remember about one another!

EQUIPMENT

- Pencils and paper
- "Hat" or paper bag for drawing names

TO PLAY

Have half of your group write their names on slips of paper, then put them in a hat. Once that is completed, ask them to line up on one side of the room. The other half of the group lines up opposite them, and draws names from the hat. In turn, each person holding a name slip gives clues as to who his partner is—**without** describing the clothes she is wearing. When someone thinks she is the one being described, she steps forward. If she is correct, she joins her partner. If not, she returns to the line, and more clues are given. Once everyone is paired off, move into an activity which requires pairs, such as Licorice Lunacy Race, or Bombs Away!

Place	Indoors
Players	Any Number
Time	5 Minutes
Energy	Moderate

The Yarn Game

The Yarn Game combines both fine- and gross-motor skills—and adds the pressure of a timed event. It's fun!

EQUIPMENT

- Two equal size balls of yarn (one each of two different colors), cut into 6" pieces

FORMATION

Split your group in half, assemble both teams on one end of the room, and assign each group a color. At the far end of the room, scatter the pieces of yarn, mingling the two colors.

TO PLAY

The rules are simple: you have 3 minutes to gather your team's color yarn pieces, and tie them together to make as long a strand of yarn as you can. Ready? Go!

At the end of three minutes, have all players stop tying. Stretch out the strands of yarn, and see which is the longer.

Ping

Place	Indoors/Outdoors
Players	Any Number
Time	10 to 15 Minutes
Energy	Moderate

Remember The Story about Ping, *by Marjorie Flack, about how Ping the duck didn't want to be the last one in line and get a whipping? In this game you don't want to be the last one back in line, either. But don't worry. We won't whip you—just eliminate you!*

EQUIPMENT

- Prepared list of things to touch
- Masking tape to demarcate the line

FORMATION

Have your entire group line up on the masking tape line you have laid out, facing one end. Note that this end is the front of the line. Call out an object which they must run to and touch, such as the far wall or the door knob. After they touch the item you call out, they are to return to this line, assembling in the order in which they return. The last person back in each round is eliminated. Continue giving items to touch until only one person remains. To keep the group on their toes, include the eliminated people as items to touch—or maybe someone who is *still* in line! You can have a lot of fun with this game!

Place	Indoors/Outdoors
Players	Any Number
Time	20 to 30 Minutes
Energy	Moderate

Mud Tub Treasure Hunt

There's nothing like the feel of mud squishing between your toes! In this game, the more you let your feet squish around, the more likely you are of finding treasure!

EQUIPMENT

- 6' round plastic wading pool
- 3 or 4 bags of top soil or potting soil, 40 pound size
- 6-8 dozen marbles
- Water supply
- Old shower curtain to place under pool, if indoors
- Old towels to place around the pool, if indoors, plus towels for drying legs
- Stopwatch or watch with second hand
- Prize(s), optional

PREPARATION

Place an old shower curtain on the floor, if indoors, and set the pool in the middle of it. Open the bags of soil and dump them into the pool. Add enough water to make the soil a slushy consistency. Scatter the marbles in the mud, stirring to submerge them, if necessary.

TO PLAY

Two players at a time remove their shoes and socks, roll up their pant legs, and hop into the pool. On the "Go!" command, players have 60 seconds to retrieve as many marbles from the muck as they can using their feet and toes, and place them outside the pool. Pairs may work cooperatively, comparing their effort against other pairs, or each person could compete individually. Either way, it's great, muddy fun!

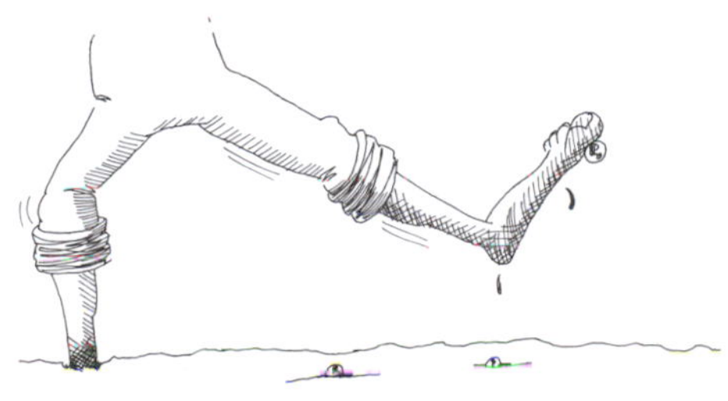

Deal The Deck

Place	Indoors
Players	20 or More
Time	5 Minutes
Energy	Moderate

This game can be played for several rounds, or used to divide your group into teams. "Let's play cards!" takes on all new meaning after your group tries Deal the Deck!

EQUIPMENT

- Playing cards, enough for each player to have one. If playing with less than 52 people, select distinctive groupings of cards. For instance with 20 players, select the tens, Jacks, Queens, Kings, and Aces of each suit.

TO PLAY

Distribute playing cards to participants. Call out a grouping, as suggested below, and watch the fur fly as participants scurry around trying to grab players they need to complete their group!

SOME SAMPLE GROUPINGS:

- Collect 4 of your type of card (all the 10's, for instance).
- Get together with everyone in your suit (a flush).
- Make three cards in a row, any suit (a straight).
- Go for a Full House, 7's wild.
- Count face cards as 10, Aces as 11. Group up to make a total of 45 points.
- Make 21 for a Black Jack.

Place	Indoors
Players	16 to 30
Time	20 to 30 Minutes
Energy	Minimal

Guess The Guest

Play this game with a fairly new group, or one that's been together awhile. You'll find out lots of interesting things about one another—and have a great time doing it!

EQUIPMENT

- Index card and pencil per player

FORMATION

Divide your group evenly in half, and have them sit randomly opposite the other team.

TO PLAY

Distribute index cards and pencils to all. Have each person secretly list 5 little-known facts about themselves. For example, "played bass drum in the college marching band," "has been to Alaska twice," "has lived in 6 states," "likes to bake," "walks fast." NOTE: Make sure each person writes his/her name at the bottom of the card. Gather the cards from each team, keeping them separate. Read a card from Team A, allowing Team B 30 seconds after each clue to guess who from Team A wrote the card. If the guest is guessed on clue 1, give the guessing team 5 points. Award 4 points if they can guess the guest in 2 clues, 3 points on clue 3, 2 points on clue 4, and 1 point if it takes all 5 clues. Even if a team guesses after a few clues, it is fun to hear all 5. It's amazing to hear the antics and adventures people have been in! After Team B has guessed a guest, give Team A a crack at one of their players. Flip flop between teams, until all the cards are used.

CHAPTER 5

Team Builders And Affirmation Activities

Often, groups of people get together for some purpose. They start out as just a bunch of individuals. At some point in their gathering together, a transformation occurs. They are no longer separate people merely assembled together; they become a TEAM! Perhaps the group you are leading (perhaps the staff itself) is still at the "gathering of familiar people" stage. The activities presented in this chapter will help your group along its progression to becoming a team.

The objective of these team building exercises is to encourage group interaction and interdependency. To put it simply, team builders are activities in which everyone's participation is required to accomplish the task at hand. Try some of these activities, and expect a transformation to occur in your group!

Group Rope Jumping

Place	Indoors/Outdoors
Players	10 to 35
Time	5 Minutes
Energy	Moderate

Yep, this game is just what the name says it is. Your group will find it a challenge to get everyone to jump in unison—but what a sense of accomplishment when they do it!

EQUIPMENT

- 50 feet of rope, or several jump ropes tied together, allowing extra length for the curving effect on the ends

FORMATION

Lay the jump rope on the ground in a straight line. Have everyone line up on one side of the rope, facing one end.

TO PLAY

Have two strong, long-armed players volunteer to be the rope turners. Give them a chance to take a few practice swings to get a feel for the length and weight of the rope. With the bulk of the rope resting on the ground, have the rest of the group line up as explained above. When everyone is ready, have the turners put the rope in motion. You may find it helpful to have one of the turners yell, "Jump!" when the rope is on the downswing. This is a challenging task, especially with larger groups, but it is sure satisfying when you can do it!

Place	Indoors/Outdoors
Players	6 to 12
Time	10 to 15 Minutes
Energy	Maximum

Team Challenge Obstacle Course

Obstacle courses can be challenging for a runner. When you ask a group of people to form a line holding hands to run through it, the challenge increases exponentially. But then, group challenges are what team building activities are all about.

EQUIPMENT

- Props to use as obstacles for the course, such as a 3 foot diameter tube (like preschools have) or a washer/dryer box with the top and bottom removed, 6 old tires or empty copy paper boxes, 6 foot to 8 foot long bench or riser, several suspended Hula-Hoops,™ etc.

PREPARATION

Set up the obstacles in an open area, allowing for 20 to 30 feet between stations. Assign spotters to stations which present possible danger.

TO PLAY

Introduce your group to the obstacle course by having an assistant demonstrate the procedures. Once everyone sees what is to be done, ask them to hold hands, forming a line. Without letting go of one another's hands (except for safety's sake), they may now attempt the obstacle course.

Evacuation

Place	Outdoors
Players	8 to 16
Time	20 to 30 Minutes
Energy	Moderate

Beam us up, Scotty, we're ready for the challenge.

EQUIPMENT

- Large water balloon
- Blind fold
- Rope, logs, and boards to use to construct suitable obstacles. (An established challenge or obstacle course is great. Otherwise, use something similar to what you set up for Team Challenge Obstacle Course.)

PREPARATION

Set up an obstacle, or series of obstacles, appropriate to the age and abilities of your group. Check them for strength and stability, to ensure the safety of your group.

THE CHALLENGE

Your group has been out exploring a previously uncharted region of innermost Outermost, a planet in the far reaches of space. Outermost has a life-supporting atmosphere, and an environment much like you find yourself in right now. The inhabitants are a friendly, but wary people, and have permitted this one visit to their planet by your party.

Up until this point in your expedition, everything has gone smoothly. You have even located a sizable nugget of balloon-ium, the only substance known to cure a deadly disease that is plaguing Earth. The amount you have been able to secure will provide immunizations for all of Earth's inhabitants for generations to come. Unfortunately, such a concentration of balloon-ium is lethal to humans if they try to carry it. Fortunately, one of your crewmen is an android, and will suffer no ill effects by carrying the bundle. (Assign someone this role, or get a volunteer.) Unfortunately, his visual circuitry has been destroyed, and he is unable to use his visual unit until he spends some time in Engineering back on board the mother ship. (Blindfold this player.)

The group is feeling good about their discovery, and about the exploration of Outermost, when disaster strikes. One of your group members (select another person), the navigator, has just sustained a broken leg, and must be carried back to the shuttle pod to receive urgent medical attention. She is the only one who knows the way back, so she must be kept alive and comfortable.

As if things couldn't get worse, all of the healthy humans drank what they perceived to be water, and have lost their ability to speak. Antidote is available at the shuttle pod, but only enough for 3 people.

Night is beginning to fall. And since nights on Outermost last for six weeks, it is imperative for your group to move as quickly and safely as possible. Your primary objective is to negotiate the obstacle course back to the shuttle pod, while safeguarding the valuable balloon-ium cargo. Good luck!

Teetering Team

Place	Outdoors
Players	10 to 25
Time	5 Minutes
Energy	Moderate

Remember how much fun it was to try to get the teeter totter to balance with you on one end, and a friend on the other? This is the same game, except here, we'll see if we can get a whole group of us balanced!

EQUIPMENT

- A **sturdy**, playground teeter-totter (see-saw, if you prefer)

TO PLAY

The only rules for this game are:

1. Everyone is included in the challenge;
2. No one's hands or feet (or elbows, knees, etc.) may touch the ground; and
3. The teeter totter should be perfectly balanced and still.

Queen Of Sheba

Place	Outdoors
Players	5 to 8
Time	5 Minutes
Energy	Moderate

This activity is especially suited for a small group. If your group is large, divide them into smaller groups, and let several teams go at once.

EQUIPMENT

- A 5 to 8 quart pot, filled 2/3 with water
- Construction cone or pylon, approximately 60 feet away to mark end line

TO PLAY

When Solomon was king, word of his incredible wisdom spread throughout the world. Many kings, rulers and nobility journeyed to visit this great, wise ruler. When they came, they brought with them caravans of precious jewels and other elaborate gifts for Solomon. The Queen of Sheba was no exception. Along with the usual gifts of finery, the Queen of Sheba brought rare and valuable spices.

If you look across the dessert, you can see the tower of King Solomon's grand castle: the orange cone. That is your destination. The Queen of Sheba, herself, must carry the pot of rare and valuable spices. She, and she alone, is the only person who may touch the pot. Since she is the queen, it is proper for her to be transported. No part of her royal body may touch the ground once the journey has begun. All the other members of the group, however, must maintain continual contact with the queen, without touching the pot itself. Since the queen wants to look her best when she meets King Solomon, it is imperative for her subjects to do their best to keep her from getting doused with "rare and valuable spices!"

Don't Axe Me!

Place	Indoors/Outdoors
Players	5 to 8
Time	10 to 15 Minutes
Energy	Maximum

This is a challenging, and exhilarating, activity. For safety's sake, make sure some of the players are actively spotting the climbers.

EQUIPMENT

- Cardboard cutout of a turkey
- Masking tape

PREPARATION

Adhere the turkey to the wall, at a height of approximately 12 to 15 feet, depending on your group's ability. It should be high enough to challenge and require their cooperative effort to retrieve, but not so high as to require unnecessary risk to retrieve.

TO PLAY

To complete your Thanksgiving dinner preparations, your group must work together to locate and retrieve the Thanksgiving turkey. No props may be used to retrieve it, only one another. Those not actively participating in its recovery should spot the others. (Spotters should alertly watch climbers with their hands raised, stand close enough to support or break a climbers fall, and remain "on duty" until all the climbers are safely back on the ground.)

Place	Indoors
Players	8 to 15
Time	5 Minutes
Energy	Moderate

Through The Hoop

Here's a simple group challenge that they'll want to try "just one more time!"

EQUIPMENT

- A Hula-Hoop™
- Stack of newspapers

FORMATION

Line your group up single file, shoulder to shoulder, an arm's length apart. Give each player a sheet or two of newspaper.

TO PLAY

Roll the Hula-Hoop™ in front of the long line of players. As it goes by, players throw a crumpled up wad of newspaper at it, attempting to throw one through the hoop. Score a point for each successful shot. Tally the points, and see if your group can do better the next time!

Spaghetti Structures

Place	Indoors
Players	9 to 18
Time	10 to 15 Minutes
Energy	Minimal

While the actual construction of the spaghetti structures is a fun and challenging activity in itself, the underlying focus of this game is small group interaction. If you leave extra materials on hand, you may find some of your group members making elaborate structures in their free time.

EQUIPMENT

- One 8 ounce box of thick spaghetti per team
- 25 wooden toothpicks per team
- 50 small gumdrops per team

FORMATION

Divide your group into teams of 3 or 4 each. Scatter these teams around the room, either on the floor, or at tables or desks.

TO PLAY

Give each team a box of spaghetti, toothpicks, and gumdrops. Tell them they have 10 minutes to build as high a structure as they can. They may use only the materials given, and the structure must be freestanding.

At the end of 10 minutes, have everyone go around and look at all the structures. Then come together and discuss what happened. Ask how they decided on how to build their structures. Did they work together well? What was frustrating about the project? What did they learn?

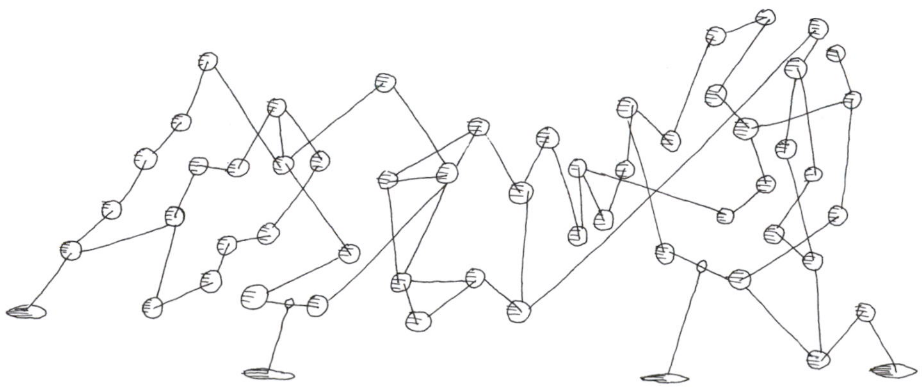

Place	Indoors/Outdoors
Players	6 to 15
Time	10 to 15 Minutes
Energy	Moderate

Tube Trip

A challenging, yet doable task that requires each person's participation and suggestions.

EQUIPMENT

- One inflated automobile tire inner tube for each group of three people

FORMATION

Divide your group into teams of three. Line teams up along the starting line.

TO PLAY

Give each group of three an inner tube. Tell them that as a team they must cross from the starting line to the finish line, which is approximately 30 feet away, without stepping directly on the ground. The inner tube may cross the 30 foot area only once.

After your group has completed the task, take some time with them to discuss how they felt doing it. What did they find was the "key" to success?

Cooperative Bean Bag Toss

Place	Indoors/Outdoors
Players	4 or More
Time	5 Minutes
Energy	Minimal

This exercise helps players to appreciate the value of others, regardless of their physical limitations.

EQUIPMENT

- 4 bean bags, or tennis balls tied in tube socks
- 2 large boxes, with holes cut in the bottom, for targets (brightly paint around the target hole to assist aiming)
- Strips of plastic wrap to tie around eyes to simulate sight loss
- Large lollipops (such as Tootsie Pops®) for each player

FORMATION

Set up two boxes, approximately 20 feet apart, as in horseshoes, with two players behind each box.

TO PLAY

One player in each pair is "blindfolded" with plastic wrap, given two bean bags, and faced away from the playing area. The other player, although sighted, must hold a lollipop in the center of her mouth. She may not touch the tosser, but may give audio commands to assist in locating the target. The visually impaired person tries tossing the bean bags into the opposite box target, as if playing horseshoes. Three points are awarded for each toss into the box, two points for landing on the top of the box, and one point for the nearest bean bag to the box. After two tosses, the other team's tosser takes her turn. Allow these players to have a few rounds, then switch roles within the two person team.

Place	Indoors
Players	8 to 15
Time	10 to 15 Minutes
Energy	Moderate

Cooperative Snacking

Communication and concern for others are the key factors in Cooperative Snacking. Let your group experience the challenge.

EQUIPMENT

- Table and chairs enough to accommodate group
- String
- Snack items and supplies, such as: crackers, peanut butter, butter knife, pitcher of drink, cups, napkins, whole oranges, carrots, peeler

FORMATION

Seat everyone at the table, and place all the snack items and supplies in the center.

TO PLAY

Tell your group you have provided a snack for them, which they need to prepare. Before they may begin, however, you have to do one more thing. With 12" to 18" lengths of string, tie the right wrist of player A to the left wrist of player B. Player B's right wrist is tied to the left wrist of player C, and so on around the table. Once this is completed, they may begin preparing, distributing, and eating their snack! Allow time afterward for discussion.

Siamese Centipede

Place	Indoors/Outdoors
Players	6 to 8
Time	5 Minutes
Energy	Moderate

Usually we take our ability to walk for granted. Not so when you're a part of a Siamese Centipede!

EQUIPMENT

- An 8-foot length of 2" x 4" lumber
- Natural or man-made obstacles, requiring some stepping up or over, slalom movements, or circling

TO PLAY

Have your group line up, straddling the board. The right half of the line should face the right end of the board, and the rest face the opposite end. Then, introduce the obstacle-laden course they are to follow, and have them negotiate the course. Allow time afterward to discuss how they felt being on the front facing end and on the backward facing end. How did they decide which end would face forward? Did they feel they completed the course successfully or efficiently?

Place	Indoors/Outdoors
Players	8 to 12
Time	10 to 15 Minutes
Energy	Moderate

People Movers

There's no "correct" way to execute this challenge. Set it before your group, and see what they come up with!

EQUIPMENT

- Two pieces of 2" x 6" x 8 foot lumber

TO PLAY

Hand your group the two boards, and tell them they must move the group from the starting point, to an end point approximately 40 feet away. The boards may make a single one-way trip. No one's feet may touch the ground once you leave the starting line, with the exception of four people. Only these four people may walk on the ground.

Follow-up this exercise with a discussion of how it went, and how they decided to do it the way they did. How were the four walkers picked, and how did they feel about it? Was safety a consideration in your option selection? Should it have been?

Affirmation Activities

Activities that encourage participants, and affirm their worth, are affirmation activities. They make effective closing or culminating activities for your group's program. When it comes to receiving encouragement, anytime is a good time, and the more often the better! But please make sure participants are sincere in their affirmations of one another.

Place	Indoors/Outdoors
Players	Any Number
Time	5 Minutes
Energy	Minimal

M&M® Mentions

A fun (and tasty!) way to affirm one another, this game is equally well-suited for a group that's recently formed, or for one that's been together for a while.

EQUIPMENT

- Sufficient number of M&M's® (or some other small candy or snack item) to allow for each person to receive 5-10

FORMATION

Grouped in a random fashion, but close enough to hear the leader's directions.

TO PLAY

Without telling them why, ask participants to take 5 to 10 M&M's,® but NOT to eat them! Once everyone has taken some M&M's,® tell them that they are to mingle around the group, and tell as many different people as they have candies something affirming. After they have encouraged someone, they may pop the corresponding M&M® into their own mouth. What good reinforcement for saying something nice to others!

Affirmation Fold-Ups

Place	Indoors
Players	Any Number
Time	5 Minutes
Energy	Minimal

An all-time biggie on the "Feel Good About Yourself" list, Affirmation Fold-Ups remind you that you are a person of value to others, and that you have lots of good qualities!

EQUIPMENT

- Blank sheet of paper (approx. 4" x 11") for each person (and leader)
- Pencil or pen for each person

FORMATION

Have your group sit in a circle on the floor, or around a table.

TO PLAY

Give each person a sheet of paper and a pencil or pen. Have them print their name at the top of the sheet. At the bottom of the sheet, they should write a one word description of themselves, then fold the bottom of the page over twice, to conceal the word. When everyone has done this, ask them to place their sheets in the middle of the circle. Each person should then select another person's paper, and write a one word (or short phrase) affirming description of that person at what is now the bottom of the page. Have them fold over the bottom again, concealing the word they just wrote, and return the sheet to the center. Participants should continue selecting one anothers' sheets until most are folded up so much that only the names show. Redistribute the sheets to their original owners, and give everyone a few minutes to look them over. If possible, allow some time for people to share the similarities and differences of their self-images, and how others perceive them.

Place	Indoors/Outdoors
Players	Any Number
Time	10 to 15 Minutes
Energy	Minimal

Affirmation Web

The Affirmation Web illustrates beautifully that everyone has value, and that we are interrelated with one another. It provides encouraging support to group members individually, as well as to the group corporately.

EQUIPMENT

- A ball of yarn or string

FORMATION

Have your group sit in a circle on the floor.

TO PLAY

The first person starts with the ball of yarn on the floor in front of her. Keeping a hold of the end, she rolls the ball of yarn to another player, and says something encouraging about that person. Positive personality qualities, something the person is good at, or perhaps something helpful or encouraging that the person has done might be mentioned. That person then keeps a hold of the yarn, and rolls the ball onto someone else, to encourage and affirm them. After everyone has had a turn (or two, if the group is small), have the group stand up, and step back one step, keeping a hold of the yarn. Have them observe how beautiful and intricate the design is, and how it took each person being included to make it so. Ask one or two people to slack their piece of yarn. Notice how the center of the web sags. If one person drops their yarn all together, notice how it effects the whole web. Use this exercise to illustrate to your group the importance of supporting and encouraging one another regularly.

Opinion Game

Place	Indoors/Outdoors
Players	Any Number
Time	5 Minutes
Energy	Moderate

The Opinion Game is a good way to begin establishing an atmosphere of trust within your group. In this game, all answers are acceptable!

EQUIPMENT

- None required, though you may find it helpful to have a list of statements written up beforehand

FORMATION

Grouped together for the directions, then players move freely within a bounded area.

TO PLAY

Show your group the two far boundaries of the playing area. The two opposite walls of your meeting room should be adequate. One wall represents the Strongly Agree side; the other, Strongly Disagree. Begin with very nonthreatening statements, such as "I like marshmallows in my hot chocolate." Group members that strongly agree with the statement move to that wall. Those strongly opposed to the statement move to the other extreme. Those group members who are somewhere in between on their opinion maneuver themselves to a place in the room that corresponds to their opinion. As you give each statement, remind participants that their opinions are valid, and that it is OK it only one person in the group likes a particular thing. We can like different things, and still be friends! Use very nonthreatening statements with new groups, until you can ascertain how accepting they really are of one another.

The following are some examples of opinion statements you might use. Be sensitive to your group, and tailor your statements to be appropriate for them.

I like marshmallows in my cocoa.
I like watching golf on TV.
I like being at the beach.
I like flying in airplanes.
I like coffee.
I love cats.
I like snow.
I like spinach.

Gifts

Place	Indoors/Outdoors
Players	10 to 20
Time	10 to 15 Minutes
Energy	Minimal

Gifts is an especially good game to play after your group has gotten to know one another well. A good imagination, and a good appreciation of one another combine to make this activity a special one for your group.

EQUIPMENT

- None (pencil and paper for each player, for variation)

FORMATION

Have your group sit in a circle, so everyone can see everyone else.

TO PLAY

Explain to your group that they are to think of a gift that they would give to each person in the group. For this game, everyone is infinitely wealthy, and capable of giving even abstract gifts. For example, someone may "give" to an adventuresome group member an expedition to Mt. Everest. A reflective, poetic member might receive eagle's wings, so they could soar on high, and gain a new perspective on life. Another player might give a summer's afternoon picnic to a friend who has a bad case of "mid-winter blues."

After you have given your group a few minutes to think what they might give one another, spotlight one player, and let other players "give" their gifts to him. Then go on to the next player, continuing until every player has received their "gifts."

VARIATION

Give each person a pencil, and a stack of paper, one piece for each other person in the group. Allow them to write down their gifts, and give others their gifts in a written fashion. Then go around the group, and let each person read aloud one or two of their most special gifts.

Bumper Stickers

Place	Indoors
Players	Any Number
Time	10 to 15 Minutes
Energy	Minimal

Even if these bumper stickers never make it to the back of a car, they provide a good outlet for self-expression.

EQUIPMENT

- Plain white self-adhesive paper, cut into 4" x 12" strips, enough for one each, plus extras
- Variety of colored permanent markers
- Scrap paper for developing designs and for protecting the table from permanent marks
- Pencils for sketching designs

TO PLAY

Lay out the materials on a table, and give the participants 5 minutes to design a bumper sticker that communicates something about themselves. You may opt to have them begin their bumper stickers with "I (HEART SYMBOL) . . ."

After participants have finished their creations, sit in a circle, and allow each person to show their bumper stickers, and explain what they are trying to communicate about themselves.

Place	Indoors
Players	12 to 24
Time	10 to 15 Minutes
Energy	Minimal

Qualities Inventory

This exercise can be a real ego booster. It reminds you of your own good qualities, and gives you perspective on how others see you.

EQUIPMENT

- Sheet of notebook paper and pencil per person

TO PLAY

Seat players in a circle or around a table, and hand out pencils and paper. At the top of the sheet, the player prints her name. Under her name, she writes three qualities she considers to be her strengths. Encourage players not to be overly modest. On the signal, each person slides her paper to the person to her right, and receives one from the left. With the new paper before her, each person reads the name on the sheet, and the qualities listed. If the quality listed is a strength of the person whose paper it is, the reader puts a check after it. If the reader can think of another positive quality that pertains to the paper's owner, she writes it in on the next line. On the signal, papers are passed again. There are no limits on the number of checks a person may give. You never run out of funds to cover these checks! (If only my bank was as generous!)

After the sheets of paper have been passed around and are returned to their original owners, allow a few minutes for people to review them. Give players an opportunity to share one or two significant qualities that received a lot of votes, or that were written in, and were particularly encouraging.

Secret Stickers

Place	Indoors
Players	Any Number
Time	10 to 15 Minutes
Energy	Minimal

This activity is sort of like a Secret Santa—only in an affirming bumper sticker form! It is especially effective with groups who have been together for a while.

EQUIPMENT

- Pencil and paper for each player
- "Hat" or box from which to draw names
- Plain white self-adhesive paper, cut in strips 4" x 12," enough for each player to have one, plus extras
- Permanent markers, in a variety of colors
- Scrap paper for design work, and to place under bumper stickers to serve as mats

TO PLAY

Have each player write her name on a slip of paper, and put it in the hat. Players take turns drawing names. With some secrecy, each player makes an affirming bumper sticker for the person she has drawn. Words, pictures, or a combination of both may be used. Allow 5 to 8 minutes, then get the group together in a circle. In turn, each player presents her bumper sticker to the person she made it for, briefly explaining its significance.

Place	Indoors/Outdoors
Players	6 to 24
Time	10 to 15 Minutes
Energy	Minimal

Self-Sculptures

You don't have to be a Michelangelo to successfully participate in Self-Sculptures. You just have to fiddle with clay, and to be willing to share a little bit about yourself.

EQUIPMENT

- Modeling clay, enough for each person to have a hockey puck size piece

TO PLAY

Sit your group in a circle, and hand each person a piece of clay. Give them 3 to 5 minutes to form the clay into something that represents one aspect of themselves. In turn, allow players to share what their sculpture is, and what it represents about themselves.

Shirt Of Arms

Place	Indoors
Players	6 to 24
Time	20 to 30 Minutes
Energy	Minimal

You are familiar with a Coat of Arms. This is the same thing, only scaled down! Have players make their designs on paper only, or have them transfer them to a plain T-shirt.

EQUIPMENT

- White construction paper cut in a T-shirt shape, enough for each person to have several if needed
- Pencils and markers or crayons for paper designs
- Permanent colored markers (if coloring on T-shirts)
- Plain T-shirts, if desired
- Newspaper to line table and place inside shirt to prevent marker from bleeding through

TO PLAY

Using the materials available, have each member of your group make a T-shirt design which represents something about who they are. The design should incorporate the artist's name in it.

Allow 10 minutes for the paper T-shirt designs. Longer time will be required to decorate a shirt. Bring the group together, and let each person display their shirt, and explain its significance.

Place	Indoors
Players	12 to 24
Time	10 to 15 Minutes
Energy	Minimal

Valentine Exchange

You needn't wait till February for this activity. Affirmations are appreciated any time of year!

EQUIPMENT

- Large construction paper hearts, enough for each player to have one
- Small plain heart stickers, or small hearts cut from plain self-adhesive paper, enough for each person to have one for each other person in the group, plus extras
- Pens or markers, enough for each person to have one

TO PLAY

Give each person a large construction paper heart, and ask him to write his name on it, in large print. Post these on a wall, or lay them out on a long table. Distribute the small heart stickers, and have each person write something "short and sweet" on each, appropriate for the others in the group. Things like "You're sweet," "I like you," "Great smile," or "You're friendly" might be used. Have them stick the hearts on the appropriate person's construction paper heart. When all the heart stickers have been distributed, let the players find their large heart, and see what Valentine messages they received.

Thanksgiving Envelopes

Place	Indoors
Players	Any Number
Time	10 to 15 Minutes
Energy	Minimal

Sometimes we need to be reminded of how much we have to be thankful for. If now is one of those times, Thanksgiving Envelopes is the activity for you!

EQUIPMENT

- A large manila mailing envelope per person
- Markers
- Pencil and paper slips for each player

TO PLAY

Give each player a mailing envelope, and have him write his name on it with a marker. Line up all the envelopes along the wall, or on a table. With pencils and paper slips in hand, participants move from envelope to envelope. At each one, they deposit a slip of paper on which they have written what *they* would be thankful for if they were the person whose name is on the envelope. For example, someone might write, "Sarah can be thankful that she's good at math" (or that she can take gymnastics lessons, that she knows how to drive, or that she doesn't wear braces any more). When everyone has contributed a slip to each envelope, distribute the envelopes to the proper players, and give them time to review them. In a circle, allow the players to share one or two slips that were particularly encouraging to them.

When we take a look at ourselves, especially our blessings, through other people's eyes, we often gain a new appreciation for what we have!

CHAPTER 6

Active Games

For a "rip-roaring" good time, try some of these games on your group! Active games are often the climax events of a recreation activities program: the crest of your programming wave. In fact, some of these activities may become so popular in and of themselves, your group might want to make them regular events!

While their intent is to allow participants to "blow off some steam," or to get some exercise, it is important for you, the leader, to maintain safety and control. Be sure to present these activities in an enthusiastic way, but do stress safe play procedures in your directions. Then get out there and enjoy some rigorous play! (Who thought working up a sweat could be so much fun!)

Wall Ball

Place	Indoors
Players	12 to 24
Time	10 to 15 Minutes
Energy	Moderate

One of my students at Penn State made up this game. After he explained the game to us, we gave it a try. We decided it was so much fun, we played it again, and again!

EQUIPMENT

- 2 tennis balls
- An enclosed area, such as a gym or racquetball court

FORMATION

Divide your group into two even teams. Each team then lines up in the middle of the gym, facing the same wall, about 15 feet from the other team. (If your group is young, have them play using the narrow width of the gym, or racquetball court. An older crowd will enjoy the challenge of playing against the far gymnasium walls.)

TO PLAY

The first person on each team is given a tennis ball. On "Go!" they each heave the ball against the gym wall in front of them, then race up and retrieve it, and toss it to the next player on their team. They remain in the spot they retrieved the ball from for the rest of the game, unmaliciously acting as obstacles for their teammates. The throw and retrieve action continues through the line for the entire team. The last player throws the ball against the front wall, retrieves it, then turns and hurls it against the opposite wall. She retrieves her second throw, and races back to her starting position in the middle of the gym. The first team finished wins that round. Allow the teams to reassemble and strategize, then go another round. The best 2 out of 3 rounds wins.

VARIATION

To add challenge to the retrieving portion of the game, scatter some sheets of paper on the floor between the team lines and the front wall. These represent land mines (or super adhesive!) and should be avoided, lest the player be forced to sprawl out on the floor there, immobilized for the rest of the game.

Place	Indoors/Outdoors
Players	20 or More
Time	10 to 15 Minutes
Energy	Maximum

Bronco Tag

This is an oldie but goodie. Play it and you'll see why!

EQUIPMENT

- None

TO PLAY

Everyone pairs up, with one of the two partners standing behind the other, their hands on the front person's waist. These pairs are the broncos—wild broncos! One of the pairs separates, with one player being "It" and the other being the ranch hand. As in any tag game, "It" tries to tag the other person, but in this game, the chased does have a way out. If the ranch hand can grab a hold of the waist of the back of one of the broncos, she can stay there. The person who had been on the front end of that bronco now becomes the ranch hand, and must try to avoid being tagged. If "It" tags the ranch hand, the players switch roles.

This is an action-packed game, as "It" tries to tag the free roaming ranch hand, who is trying desperately to link onto the back of one of the broncos, who are doing their darnedest to steer clear of the action, so they don't have to go racing around the playing area! An active game for ranch hands and broncos alike!

Kickball For All

Place	Indoors/Outdoors
Players	20 to 40
Time	20 to 30 Minutes
Energy	Moderate

Kickball for All, a variation of the standard game, keeps everyone actively participating in the game. No bench warmers in this game!

EQUIPMENT

- Playground or soccer ball
- Bases (for variation)
- Large, open playing area or field

TO PLAY

Divide your group into two even teams: the outfielders and the team at bat. One of the outfielders or one of the leaders pitches the ball to the first kicker, as in a "normal" game of kickball. Once the ball is kicked, however, the game departs from normalcy, and transforms into an all-players involved frenzy! As soon at the kicker gives the ball a boot, she runs around her *team*, which has lined itself up in at tight line, behind the batter's box. Every lap run around the team is one run scored for her team. Have the team yell out the runs as the batter circles them.

Meanwhile, back in the outfield, someone has fielded the ball. That person raises the ball above his head, and the rest of the outfield scurries over to line up behind him. The ball is passed from player to player, above their heads. When it reaches the last person in line, they yell "STOP!" This is the signal for the runner to stop, and tally the number of completed laps made around their team. Since there are no fly ball outs, and no strikeouts, decide in advance how many "at bats" constitute a half inning, then switch sides. There's no dozing in the outfield, or sitting on your hands on the bench in this game. If you're playing Kickball for All, you're *all* playing!

VARIATION

Bases may be used, with kickers running around them,instead of around their teammates. Runners continue racing around the bases until the outfield yells "STOP!" If a player makes it past home plate before being told to stop, she stays on that base until the next player kicks her in, thus scoring more than one run for her team. If a player does not get back to home on her turn, she stays on base, until the next player kicks her in, but only scores one run for her team. Or, if you like higher math (and higher scores), give the team a point for each *base* run. Remember: there is no rule that you have to use a standard ball field. The closer the bases, the more runs each player gets to score!

12 Minute Kickball

Place	Indoors/Outdoors
Players	18 to 40
Time	10 to 15 Minutes
Energy	Maximum

Even if you have an extended period of play, this is a great game. The timed innings really keep the game moving and the players hustling!

EQUIPMENT

- 4 bases
- Kickball
- Pencil and paper to keep score
- Stopwatch, or watch with second hand

FORMATION

Split your group into two teams. Have one team start as fielders, the other starting at bat.

TO PLAY

12 Minute Kickball consists of three timed innings: the first, 3 minutes long; the second, 2 minutes; and the third, 1 minute long. Have a leader be all-time pitcher, or have the offensive team supply one. Players must move as quickly as possible, so as many players as can, get a turn at bat. Remind fielders of the Golden Rule: field quickly for the other team, and they'll field the ball quickly for you. The offensive team scores one point for *each* base a player reaches. If someone kicks a fly ball that is caught, the team gets an out. After 3 outs, the bases are cleared, but the team remains at bat until time is called. When time is called, the teams change positions on the field, and the clock begins ticking again!

Place	Indoors/Outdoors
Players	20 to 40
Time	20 to 30 Minutes
Energy	Moderate

Mat Ball

Stealing bases is an exciting part of baseball-type games. In Mat Ball, sneaking off to the next base when you're ready is what makes this game so much fun!

EQUIPMENT

- Playground or soccer ball
- Home plate, plus three 4' x 6' mats (or tape to mark off that area for each base)
- Large, open area to play in, such as a gym or playing field

TO PLAY

This game is played much like kickball, with fly balls, and throwing the ball to basemen to get runners out. The difference is that a runner is not forced to move on to the next base. As many players as choose to may accumulate on a base. Individuals may leave in any order (or all at once!) to go on to the next base, which keeps the base players on their toes!

Frisbee™ Baseball

Place	Indoors/Outdoors
Players	20 to 30
Time	20 to 30 Minutes
Energy	Moderate

Hitting a hurled ball with a stick might be a frustrating experience for some in your group. Frisbee™ Baseball gives your players a much better chance of getting on first, and around to the other bases. Minimal frustrations, maximum fun. That's what this game's all about!

EQUIPMENT

- Large open area to serve as the ball field
- Bases
- Frisbee™

FORMATION

Group is divided into two teams. The outfielders take positions as in baseball, but with no pitcher needed.

TO PLAY

This game is run as a regular baseball game, with several variations. The person at bat starts with the Frisbee,™ and throws it when and how she likes. There are no automatic outs on "fly balls." Runners may be tagged out, or forced out by having the Frisbee™ on the base they are forced to run to.

After 3 outs, or a predetermined number of runners, the two teams switch places. Continue playing until you've reached the desired number of innings, or until the game is called because of darkness!

Place	Indoors
Players	20 to 40
Time	10 to 15 Minutes
Energy	Moderate

The Rescue Rudolph Snowball Fight

Excitement runs high as the Christmas holidays approach. Why not take advantage of it with this game? A combination of Capture the Flag, and Run the Gauntlet, this game may be the favorite game at your center this December.

EQUIPMENT

- A red bandana, or other red object to represent Rudolph
- Several days worth of newspapers
- Boundary markers (cones or tape)

PREPARATION

Lay out the playing field with two end goals, and an open area between, as illustrated below:

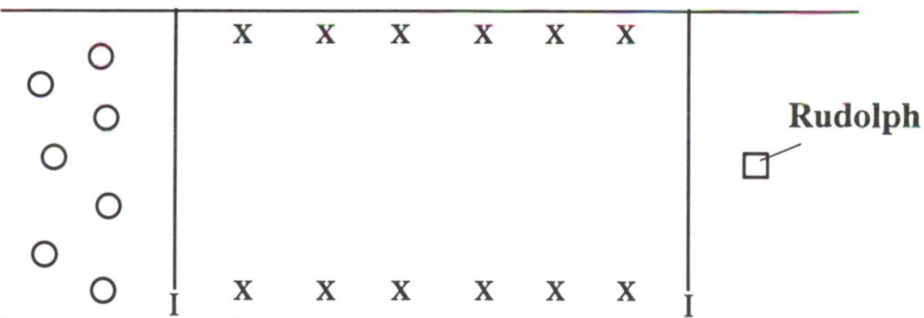

X = Bah Hum Bugs

O = Elves

TO PLAY

Divide your group into two teams: the Elves, and the Bah Hum Bugs. The Bah Hum Bugs have captured Rudolph, and confined him to a cave far from the North Pole. The Elves, of course, feel an obligation to rescue poor Rudolph, so he can guide Santa's sleigh. Those rascally Bah Hum Bugs have armed themselves with snowballs (crumpled pages of newspaper), and are ready to thwart the efforts of those enthusiastic elves. On "Go!" the elves try to run from their base (the North Pole), through the Land of the Bah Hum Bugs, retrieve Rudolph, and return him to a grateful Santa—all without getting stunned by a snowball. If an elf gets hit by a snowball at any time, he returns to the North Pole for some quick nurturing, before heading back out into the storm. Rudolph, if he was on his escape when his elf got hit, must return to the Cave of Confinement. Once Rudolph is reunited with Santa and all his reindeer friends, switch roles, so the Bah Hum Bugs get a chance at Santa's good side, too!

Ribbon Rip-Off

Place	Indoors/Outdoors
Players	Any Number
Time	5 Minutes
Energy	Maximum

This is a great, high energy game of cat-and-mouse, where each person is both cat and *mouse at the same time!*

EQUIPMENT

- Two (2) one-foot-long pieces of yarn or ribbon per player
- Masking tape
- Boundary markers

TO PLAY

Each player is given two pieces of ribbon, which they tape to the top of the outside of their shoulders. Each shoulder should have a ribbon, and the ribbon should be taped on one end, so most of the ribbon can dangle down freely. Assemble your group *en masse* in the designated playing area. On the "Go!" command, players race around, trying to rip-off one another's ribbons. As long as a player is wearing a ribbon, she may continue to play. Once both ribbons have been removed, the player must retire to the sidelines. As the number of active players dwindles, the boundary markers should be correspondingly compressed. The last player left, and the player who has gathered the most ribbons from others, could be awarded some appropriate prize, say, a strand of shoestring licorice!

Swat

Place	Indoors/Outdoors
Players	12 or More
Time	10 to 15 Minutes
Energy	Moderate

This game is played similarly to "Duck, Duck, Goose," but is much more exciting!

EQUIPMENT

- A section of newspaper rolled and taped (the swatter)
- A stool, chair, or similar small, elevated surface

FORMATION

Have your group stand in a circle, with the stool in the middle. With a small group, players should be at least 15 feet from the center; larger groups should stand further away.

TO PLAY

Choose someone from your group to be "It." Have her walk around *inside* the circle, with the swatter in hand. At an opportune time, "It" swats someone on the legs. Without a moment's hesitation, "It" races back to the center of the circle, sets the swatter on the stool, and zips off to assume the victim's place in the circle. Meanwhile, the swat victim rushes to the stool to take possession of the swatter, to try to swat "It" before she returns to the circle. If he is successful, he may return to his place in the circle, and "It" must go another round. If, however, "It" did manage to slip back into the circle unscathed, the swat victim becomes "It" for the next round. Although this seems straightforward enough, the thing about tubular swatters and small surfaced stools is that things don't always stay put. And in this game, if the swatter falls off the stool, "It" must come back to the center to place it back on the top. This can make for some interesting cat-and-mouse action, especially if an agitated swat victim happens to be looming around the stool, ready to grab the swatter and return the "favor!"

Place	Outdoors (Wooded)
Players	10 to 20
Time	20 to 30 Minutes
Energy	Moderate

Secret Summons

Secret Summons is a hide-and-seek variation that allows (actually, encourages) the hiders to defend one another from long-term jail sentences.

SETTING

A large, outdoor area which has many places for players to hide is needed for this game. Within it, there should be a small, clearly defined "jail" area, which can easily be seen from the hiding places.

TO PLAY

"It" stands in the jail, and counts to 100 (or whatever is needed to give the group ample time to hide). Each person selects a hiding place, making sure he can see the jail directly or with minor repositioning from his position. Players may not go into buildings.

Once finished counting, "It" begins roaming around, looking for other players. When she spots someone, she calls out the person's name (or accurately describes their clothes), and declares exactly where they are hiding. The discovered person walks directly and unescorted to the jail.

When the prisoner reaches the jail, he calls out loudly, "Free Me!" Any other uncaptured player can then secretly summon the captured player by making visual contact, and beckoning to him with their finger(s). The prisoner has then been freed, but may choose to remain safely in jail until he can safely sneak to a hiding place without being spotted by "It." If an escaping prisoner is seen making his get-away, "It" may identify the player again, and the prisoner must return to jail, and call for another secret summons. It is "It's" job to capture players, and to make sure those in jail stay there.

Play continues until "It" captures all the players, or until Mom calls you in for supper!

VARIATION

For a larger group, try playing with more than one "It."

Black Panther

Place	Outdoors (Wooded)
Players	8 to 15
Time	20 to 30 Minutes
Energy	Moderate

We spent many a summer's eve playing this hide-and-seek type game. It is especially thrilling as twilight approaches, though extra care must be taken then to avoid tripping over roots, running into branches, or stumbling upon the Black Panther unexpectedly! Even mixed aged groups will find this game fun.

EQUIPMENT

- Base, such as a large tree
- A large outdoor playing area with many places to hide

TO PLAY

Select one person to be the first Black Panther. Then, the Black Panther stealthily sneaks off to find a hiding place, while the rest of the group stands at the base, *eyes closed*, counting to 100. When they reach 100, players will move about, trying to discover the Black Panther's whereabouts. While the Black Panther *does* want to catch players, it may be in her best interest to not jump out too soon. By waiting, Black Panther may be able to lure unsuspecting prey further from base. As soon as a player does spot the Black Panther, he screams out loudly, "Black Panther!" This bloodcurdling scream (often delivered with realistic urgency!) is the signal for all players to hightail it back to base. As they scramble back to reach safety, the Black Panther tries to tag as many players as she can.

Once the Black Panther has pounced on her prey, and calmness has returned to the flock, select a new Black Panther, and play again—if your nerves can take it!

Place	Indoors/Outdoors
Players	12 to 20
Time	20 to 30 Minutes
Energy	Moderate

Steal The Broom Hockey

As the name implies, this is a combination of Steal the Bacon and Broom Hockey. And it's a lot of fun!

EQUIPMENT

- A large, open playing area, such as a small gym, or game area, or field
- Two **sturdy** brooms
- Two chairs
- A rag or old towel tied into a ball

PREPARATION

Place a chair at each end of the playing area. These will serve as goals. Set the rag ball in the middle of the playing area, equidistant from each team. Brooms should be placed on either side of the rag ball, bristles toward it, handles pointing at the goals.

TO PLAY

For maximum fairness and fun for all, divide your group into two even teams. (You might try lining the group up by height, and then have them count off by 2's.) Line up the two teams on opposite sides of the playing area, with the biggest players on the right end of each line, as they face the middle. Have each team number off, and remember their own numbers! As in Steal the Bacon, the leader calls out a number, and the players from each team with that number race to the center of the playing area. From here, the game switches over to Broom Hockey, as each player grabs a broom and tries to sweep the rag ball under their team's chair. A successful goal scores a point for their team. Brooms and the rag ball are returned to their original center positions, and another number is called.

Play continues until all the numbers have been called, time runs out, or the brooms disintegrate into a pile of straw and stick fragments!

Beat The Ball

Place	Indoors/Outdoors
Players	10 to 25
Time	5 Minutes
Energy	Moderate

A great racing game, Beat the Ball can be played most any time or place. It is an excellent way to remedy those "I'm tired of sitting" blues!

EQUIPMENT

- A tennis ball, or something similar

FORMATION

Everyone (except the first runner) joins hands and forms a circle, stepping back to make it as large as possible. Once the circle is fully extended, players drop their hands to their sides.

TO PLAY

Someone in the circle starts with the tennis ball in her hand. The runner stands behind the person with the ball. On the signal to go, the runner begins running around the outside of the circle in a clockwise fashion. The ball is simultaneously passed from person to person along the inside of the circle. The race is to see which returns to the original starting position first: the ball or the runner! You may chose to run the race having the ball make one, two, or even three circuits, depending on the size of the group, time allowed, and the enthusiasm of the runner!

Place	Indoors/Outdoors
Players	16 to 30
Time	20 to 30 Minutes
Energy	Maximum

A.T.B. (All Touch Ball)

This is an excellent, challenging game! Every player is critical to the success of their team (and you get quite a workout as well!)

EQUIPMENT

- Volleyball, or similar sized ball
- 2 cardboard boxes (like copier paper boxes) for goals
- Pinnies or arm bands for both teams, if possible, or some other way to distinguish them
- A referee whistle is also helpful

FORMATION

Form two teams. Each team scatters itself around the play area, which should be a full basketball court size or larger. Goals are placed at opposite far corners of the playing field. Each team defends one of these goals. Any player may move anywhere in the entire field, except directly in/over the goal they are defending. A player from each team should be in the center of the field for the opening jump ball.

TO PLAY

The game begins with a jump ball at mid-field. The team that controls the ball must maneuver the ball across the field to score a goal. The ball may be passed or handed over after a maximum of three steps, but must remain in the control of the possessing team. A goal is scored when the ball touches down inside the boundary of the goal—**but** before a goal may be attempted, **every** person on the offensive team must have touched the ball! If the other team should gain possession of the ball by even one player, the slate is wiped clean, and each player must again touch the ball for a goal to be attempted. If an opposing team member touches the ball as it is being passed, but does not fully gain control of the ball, play continues with only team members not having touched the ball needing to do so before attempting to score. Once a goal is scored, play is resumed with a jump ball. Jump balls may also be used to settle disputes during the course of play.

WARNING

This game has the potential to become very aggressive. Institute a "Freeze!" command, whereby all players freeze when the whistle is blown, or the command given. Be sure to remind players that the goal is to have fun, and to encourage one another. If you find the teams to be rather lopsided, shuffle the teams to make them more evenly matched.

Play continues until one team reaches a certain score. Watch for fatiguing players: tired players make for injured or irritable players. If your group is not used to being so physically active, you may want to end sooner ("Next goal wins!").

Don't be surprised if this becomes one of your group's favorite games!

Place	Indoors/Outdoors
Players	12 to 30
Time	10 to 15 Minutes
Energy	Moderate

Samurai Soda Swatters

This is a great "pick-up" game after a picnic or party: anytime you empty a two-liter soda bottle! (And chances are good you'll find some volunteers to give their socks to roll up and use as foam ball substitutes!)

EQUIPMENT

- A one- or two-liter plastic soda bottle
- 3-5 softball sized foam balls

FORMATION

Have your group form a circle, about 30 feet in diameter.

TO PLAY

Give your Samurai the plastic soda bottle, and have him stand in the center of the circle. Hand the foam balls to people in the circle. On "Go," they may attempt to hit the Samurai with the ball. He, of course, does his very best to defend himself by thwarting the incoming projectiles with his "sword." Award him one point for each successful defensive hit. If, however, he is hit by one of the balls, he must change places with the thrower. During the course of the game, members of the circle may step inside the circle to retrieve a dead ball. However, they must return to the circle before throwing it.

To add additional challenge to the game, have players hold their hands behind their backs, so the Samurai warrior doesn't know from where to expect the ball.

Pull Over

Place	Indoors/Outdoors
Players	Any Number
Time	5 Minutes
Energy	Maximum

A classic game of conquest, power, and finesse.

EQUIPMENT

- None, except for a line on the ground or floor

FORMATION

Divide the group in half. Have each team stand facing the other team, with the line between them. Players should stand about 18 inches from the line.

TO PLAY

On the "Go!" signal, players begin attempting to pull opposing players to their side of the line. Once pulled over, players instantly switch alliance to the team whose side they are now on. Players continue to pull and be pulled over the line, until all players are pulled onto one side, or they surrender fatigued!

Place	Indoors/Outdoors
Players	Pairs
Time	5 Minutes
Energy	Moderate

Defend De Fruit (or, Leave My Lemon Alone!)

A game of skill, strategy, and balance, all for the sake of preserving your lemon!

EQUIPMENT

- Two large spoons per person
- One lemon per person

TO PLAY

Each player receives two spoons: one empty one, and one with a lemon resting in its "bowl." On "Go," each player tries to use his empty spoon to knock his opponent's lemon to the ground, while trying to keep his own safely cradled in his other spoon. Challenge your partner to best 2 out of 3, then move on to a new partner.

Taunt The Tiger

Place	Indoors/Outdoors
Players	12 to 24
Time	5 Minutes
Energy	Moderate

Nothing socially redeeming about this game: it's just fun to play!

EQUIPMENT

- Masking tape to mark off a 5' to 6' diameter circle

FORMATION

Select one player to be the tiger, and have him stand in the center of the circle. All the other players stand around the outside of the circle.

TO PLAY

The tiger, who is confined to his circle, is considered very dangerous. He has been known to devour small children (and people much like those in your group) in a single bite. While attempts to eradicate this menace have failed, villagers continue to taunt the tiger, in hopes that this will drive the beast away. Villagers may poke and prod the tiger, but if he whirls around and tags you, you are wounded, and must sit out the rest of the round while you receive "medical attention." If the tiger can successfully grab you and pull you into the circle, you become the new tiger. At this point, all injured villagers are fully recovered, and healthy enough to taunt the new tiger.

Place	Indoors
Players	32 to 60
Time	10 to 15 Minutes
Energy	Maximum

4-Way Balloon Bust Up

This game may look like a free-for-all, but there's a lot of team strategy going on. (And a lot of fun to be had!)

EQUIPMENT

- 9" balloons, inflated, of 4 different colors, so each person has one
- 4 very large trash bags
- Masking tape to mark team end lines

FORMATION

Divide your group into four even teams, and assemble them in a large square, one team per side. (Consider playing the *Balloon Blow Up* game, page 121, to inflate the balloons.) Each team should select one player to act as goalie, who is given a trash bag.

TO PLAY

All players place their balloons in the center of the square. Mix them up, so there is an even distribution of colors. Each team has a two-purpose goal: to preserve as many of their color balloons as possible, while trying to eliminate as many opposition balloons as they can. To preserve their own balloons, players move their balloons soccer style (no hands or arms) to their team's goalie. The goalie may use her hands to pick up balloons and place them in the trash bag, but she must stay in the center of her team's end line. Eliminating opposition balloons is done by stomping them.

When all the inflated balloons have been removed from the center of the square, round 1 is over. Each goalie counts how many of her team's balloons remain, as she returns them from her bag to the play area in the center of the square. A team must have at least one balloon still inflated in order to move on to the next round. Rounds continue until only one team remains with an inflated balloon.

Bandana Ball

Place	Indoors/Outdoors
Players	12 or More
Time	5 Minutes
Energy	Moderate

The trick of this game is knowing how to catch the bandana properly. With practice, your group could keep it moving flawlessly for hours!

EQUIPMENT

- One tennis ball
- Two bandanas, or one large 24" x 24" one

PREPARATION

Lay the tennis ball on one bandana. Tie it into the bandana in such a way as to leave a "tail." Tie the second bandana to the tail, and tie a second knot towards the other end of the second bandana. Leave approximately 8 inches of space between the two knots.

TO PLAY

Have players stand in a circle, or in two parallel lines, 20 feet apart. Players toss the ball back and forth, catching it between the lower two knots. Any player catching it above or below this area, or on the knots, is eliminated from play. Continue tossing until a champion remains.

VARIATION

Instead of eliminating players, make Bandana Ball a cooperative effort: see how many times your group can toss it successfully. Or, pair up your group and give each pair a bandana ball. Have pairs toss it back and forth, widening their distance apart with each toss. Set up a Bandana Ball tournament! The possibilities are endless!

Place	Indoors
Players	16 to 50
Time	20 to 30 Minutes
Energy	Maximum

Balloon Batting Battle

Who would have thought balloons and paper plates could produce such fun? (And so much sweat!)

EQUIPMENT

- Several inflated balloons (see *Balloon Blow Up* game, page 121)
- Cheap paper plates, enough for each player to have 2 or 3
- Two Hula-Hoops™
- String to suspend Hula-Hoops™
- Pinnies or arm bands to distinguish teams

FORMATION

Suspend the Hula-Hoops™ on opposite ends of the playing area. (Basketball hoops work well, for instance.) Break your group into two even teams, and give them pinnies or arm bands, and paper plates to use to bat the balloon. Team players scatter themselves around the playing area, with a player from each team in the center for a jump ball to initiate the action.

TO PLAY

Play begins with a jump ball (balloon) in mid-field. Team players try to bat the balloon with their paper plates, moving them across the playing area to their goal. Paper plates are to be used to *bat* the balloon, not to cradle it or carry it. When the balloon passes through the suspended Hula-Hoop,™ the team is awarded a point. Play resumes with another jump ball at center.

Poison Papers

Place	Indoors/Outdoors
Players	20 or More
Time	5 Minutes
Energy	Maximum

Poison Papers is a "Get Your Neighbor Before He Gets You" game that's sure to get good reviews from your group!

EQUIPMENT

- Several sheets of newspaper
- Masking tape
- Chalk, if playing on a paved surface outdoors

PREPARATION

Tape several sheets of newspaper to the floor, making a 24"-30" square.

FORMATION

Have your group stand in a circle, holding hands, around the Poison Paper, and count off by 2's.

TO PLAY

It's the 1's against the 2's in a pushing, pulling battle to make players from the opposite team touch the Poison Paper. Once any part of your body touches the Poison Paper, you must leave the circle. Hands are rejoined, and play continues until only members of one team remain!

Potato Poaching

Place	Indoors/Outdoors
Players	12 to 24
Time	5 Minutes
Energy	Moderate

Potatoes are usually a readily available commodity, but not in this game. If you want potatoes, ya' gotta' poach 'em!

EQUIPMENT

- 2 or 3 medium to large potatoes
- Masking tape or chalk to mark circles

FORMATION

Place the potatoes inside a 3 foot diameter circle. Mark another circle around this first one, with a diameter of 9 feet.

TO PLAY

Two players volunteer, or are selected, to guard the potatoes. They must stay within the bounds of the larger circle. All the other players stand around the outside of the circle, awaiting an opportunity to pounce in and poach a potato! The Spud Guards, of course, do their best to prevent poaching, and grab at anyone they can reach. If a Spud Guard grabs you, you are out of the game until someone else successfully poaches a potato. When this happens, new Spud Guards are commissioned, the potatoes repotted, and the poachers prepare to perpetrate!

Lumberjack Contest

Place	Indoors
Players	20 or More
Time	20 to 30 Minutes or More
Energy	Maximum

We saw a great Lumberjack Show at the North Carolina State Fair last fall. I didn't think we could duplicate every event, but I did think it was an event worth adapting for use by fun-loving folks like ourselves! Aaah, Yo, Ho!

EQUIPMENT

- Carrots of equal size, two per team
- Carrot peelers, two per team
- "Logs" of equal length and diameter, one per team (They need not be big, as long as all are about the same size. Four inch diameter fireplace logs are adequate)
- Plastic knives, two per team
- Loaves of French bread, 3 foot long size, one per team
- Frying pan and pancake turners, one set per team
- Oven mitts, one per team
- Frozen pancakes, one per team
- Pretzel rods, one per player, plus extras
- Jar of peanut butter
- Poster board cut into 1" x 9" strips, enough for each person to get two strips
- Stapler with staples
- Markers

FORMATION

Divide your group into even teams of 8 to 12 players each. Have each lumberjack crew select an appropriate team name. Some events will require 2 contestants per team. Others will involve the entire lumberjack crew.

TO PLAY

"X" THROWING

Give each participant two strips of poster board, and ask them to write their names on them with the markers. Staple the two pieces together, forming an "X," (or axe, get it?!) When contestants are ready, have each team line up in turn to do the "X" throw. The top three finishers from each team will compete together in the final round. The "X" which goes the farthest wins 50 points for their crew! Second place finisher earns 40 points, third 30, and so on.

LOG PEELING

Each lumberjack crew puts forth its best two log peelers. Once the contestants have stepped forward, hand each one a carrot and a carrot peeler. On the "Go!" command, lumberjacks begin, feverishly peeling the outer layer of carrot. The first contestant to successfully clean his carrot lets out an enthusiastic "Aaah, Yo Ho!" and earns his team 50 points. Second place finisher earns 40, and so on.

TEAM LOG ROLLING CONTEST

Teams line up relay style for this event. In front of each team place a log. In turn, each member of each team must roll the log with her feet, to a turning point 30 to 50 feet away, then roll it back to the next player on her team.

2-MAN SAWING CONTEST

Each team puts forward a pair of players to compete in the 2-man sawing contest. Contestants may be both male, both female, or one of each, as the team decides. Each pair kneels opposite each other, with a loaf of French bread and two plastic knives between them. On the "Go!" signal, each pair picks up their knives, and begins cutting through the loaf of bread. The first pair to saw through the loaf, dividing it into a 3 foot long top and a 3 foot long bottom wins 50 points for their team! (Deduct points for cut fingers!)

FLAP JACK FLIP

Again, teams line up relay style. This event is a good one for those most important members of any logging crew: the cooks! The first cook on each crew is given an oven mitt, a turner, and a frying pan with a flapjack in it. On "Go," each cook scoops up the pancake, flips it at least 2 feet in the air, catches it, and passes all the utensils to the next person in line. After the last person in line has completed the task, she runs triumphantly to the front of the line with fry pan in hand, and her whole team sits down, shouting, "Aaah, Yo Ho!"

INDIVIDUAL LOG ROLLING CONTEST

Line up each team so they make a side of a polygon (many sided shape). Hand each player a whole pretzel rod, which has a dab of peanut butter on one end. On the "Go!" command, each player sticks the clean end of the pretzel rod in his mouth. Then, by only using his mouth and tongue, he must maneuver it so the peanut butter end is now in his mouth. The first player to successfully do this without breaking (or eating!) his pretzel earns 50 points for his team!

CHAPTER 7

Relays

In Chapter 3, we discussed ideas for choosing teams. Now that we've got them, let's run some relay races!

Relay races can be a fun way to build group spirit, while enjoying each other's company. Present your relay races with more emphasis on the fun, and less on the competition, to keep enjoyment levels high. Be sure to demonstrate how you want the group to perform the event, so everyone has a clear picture of what they are to do. Or have an assistant demonstrate while you act as commentator, giving elaborate (and humorous?!) descriptions of each step to be followed. **Get Ready** the props. **Get Set** the group. **Go!**

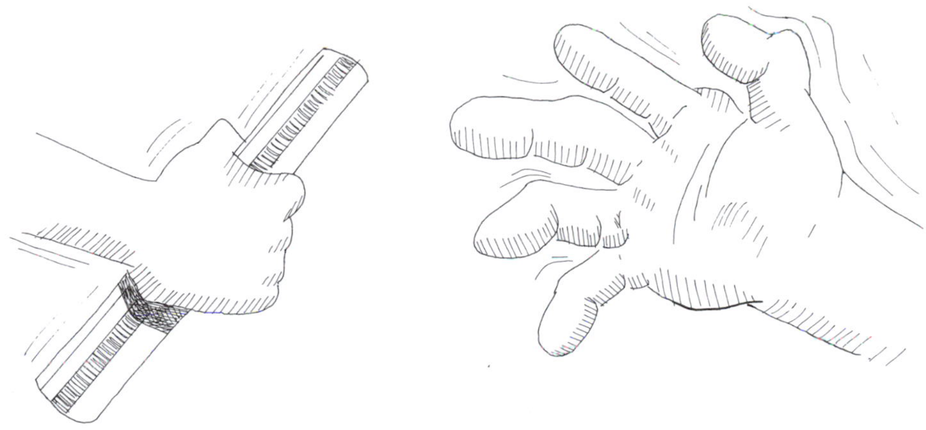

Sunbathers Relay

Place	Indoors/Outdoors
Players	12 or More
Time	5 Minutes
Energy	Maximum

It may be snowy out, but your group can step back into summer with this relay. The only problem may be getting them to stop!

EQUIPMENT

- One beach chair or folding chair per team
- A pair of sturdy sunglasses per team

FORMATION

Set your group up relay style, in even teams of 6 to 10 players each.

TO PLAY

The first person in each line is given a beach chair and a pair of sunglasses. On "Go," this person runs about 50 feet to the predetermined spot on the "beach," sets up the chair, sits in it, puts on the sunglasses, leans back, crosses his legs, and yells "I love the sun!" Once that is all said and done, he stands up, removes the sunglasses, folds the chair, and races back to the next person in line, who takes the chair and the sunglasses, and hightails it out to his vacation on the beach. The first team to have every player finish wins—a bottle of sunscreen!

Place	Indoors
Players	12 or More
Time	5 Minutes
Energy	Moderate

Domino Relay

Watching a row of dominoes fall is always fascinating. But when teams race to set them up first, you've got some real fun viewing on hand!

EQUIPMENT

- 3 to 5 dominoes per player

FORMATION

Divide your group into even teams of 6 to 8 players each, and have them line up relay style. Pass out domino pieces so each participant has the same number of pieces.

TO PLAY

In turn, each team member runs to the designated end line, and carefully places her domino pieces in an upright position. (You know, domino style!) When the first person returns to the line, she touches off the next person, who adds his pieces to his teammate's line. And so the race continues until everyone has added her dominoes to her team's line. (**NOTE:** If anyone knocks the dominoes down, she must set them back up before returning to the team.) The honor of touching off the dominoes is left to the first person in line. She makes a return trip to the end line, sets the domino effect in motion, and races back to her team amid the claps and cheers of her teammates.

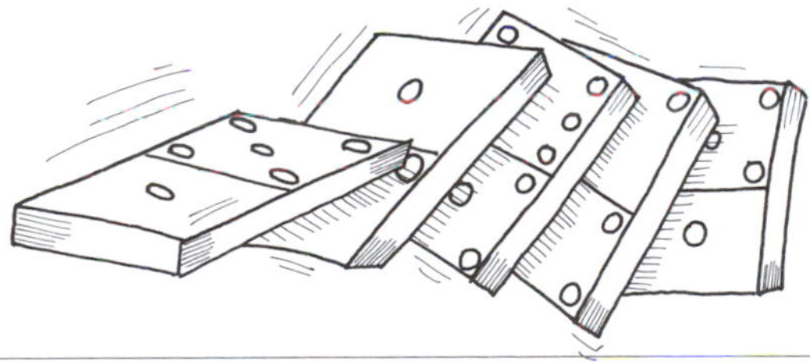

Sleigh Ride

Place	Indoors
Players	12 or More
Time	5 Minutes
Energy	Maximum

You can almost hear those sleigh bells jingling as the teams go racing by. But the squeals of laughter and grunts of effort would surely drown them out anyway!

EQUIPMENT

- A large cardboard box for each team (banana or apple boxes from the grocery store work well)

FORMATION

Divide your group into even teams of 6 to 8 players each. Members of each team pair up for this race.

TO PLAY

The first couple on each team is given an open box, into which one of them places his posterior. The other partner stands in front of the box, facing forward, and grabs hold of her partners ankles. When all the teams have hitched up their sleighs, the leader cracks the whip (or simply yells "GO!"), and the race is on! The sleighs race to a turnaround point 50 feet away. Horse and rider trade positions for the return trip to the next anxious horse and rider pair. The first team to exercise all their horses wins.

Place	Indoors
Players	12 or More
Time	5 Minutes
Energy	Maximum

Chariot Races

Who says the great civilizations of the past are dead? With a few boxes and some willing participants, you can reenact one of the classic events of the Roman Empire: Chariot Races!

EQUIPMENT

- A large, solid-bottomed box for each team (like an apple or orange box from the grocery store)
- Cones, or something to mark the turning point

PREPARATION

Across from each team, place a cone or similar marker approximately 50 feet away, to show the turning point. Open the boxes, and place the lids under the bottoms of the boxes for reinforcement.

TO PLAY

Each team divides into groups of threes: one chariot driver, and two horses. The first chariot driver sits in the box, with his knees or bottom on the bottom, and extends his arms to grab a rein (arm) of each of the two "horses." Before the royal emperor (the leader) gives the command for the race to commence, he should be sure to warn his subjects to race in a controlled manner: chariot drivers are to remain *in* their boxes, not catapulted across the coliseum as they round the turning point. The race concludes when every team member has had an opportunity to drive a chariot (or someone floods the arena for the Roman battleship contest!).

Cocoon The Platoon

Place	Indoors/Outdoors
Players	16 or More
Time	5 Minutes
Energy	Moderate

Here's a good way to get your group closer together—literally!

EQUIPMENT

- An unstarted roll of masking tape per team

FORMATION

Divide your group into even teams with 8 to 12 in each. Have each team line up relay style, fairly close to the person in front of them, with everyone facing forward.

TO PLAY

Place identical, new rolls of masking tape on the floor in front of the first person in each line. On "Go," the first person in each line picks up the roll of tape, and begins removing a strip of tape. They stick the first foot or two of the roll across their stomachs, and pass the roll to the person behind them, who continues passing, and unrolling the tape to the next one in line. When the tape reaches the last person in line, she passes the roll behind her back, sticking a stretch of it to her back, then sends the roll back up the line, on the opposite side. This cocooning of the team continues until the roll of tape is used up. The first team to raise up an empty tape tube gives a cheer! (Now that everyone is together, why not try a *Caterpillar Obstacle Course,* described on the next page?)

Place	Indoors/Outdoors
Players	16 or More
Time	5 Minutes
Energy	Moderate

Caterpillar Obstacle Course

This game is a natural continuation of the last one. Not only is it a lot of fun, it also encourages cooperation among group members.

EQUIPMENT

- Teams of 8 to 12, who are cocooned together (see: *Cocoon the Platoon*)
- Props to serve as obstacles, such as chairs, Hula-Hoops,™ cones, trees, or poles to circle around. Have at least as many obstacle stations as you have teams

PREPARATION

Space obstacles around your playing area with plenty of room between them. Obstacles should be appropriate for the age and abilities of your participants. And keep in mind they will be "stuck" together as they perform these tasks. Having each person in turn sit on a chair, climb through a suspended Hula-Hoop,™ or take a sip of water from a water fountain, may be plenty challenging for a human caterpillar.

TO PLAY

Have each caterpillar start at a different station along the obstacle course. Explain and demonstrate how they are to perform each task, and show them the direction in which they should move from one station to the next. "Require" caterpillars to keep their masking tape skin in tact as they go. First group back gets to metamorphose into a butterfly!

Recycling Rangers Relay

Place	Indoors/Outdoors
Players	12 or More
Time	10 to 15 Minutes
Energy	Moderate

This exercise could be a great follow-up activity to a recycling lesson, or as a means of educating and encouraging your group to recycle household items. Reuse Every Container You Can. Love our Earth

EQUIPMENT

- A recycling bin or cardboard box per team
- Lots of recyclables, such as newspapers, soda cans, empty milk jugs, metal cans, plastic and paper grocery bags
- Lots of nonrecyclables, such as foam cups or produce trays, empty shampoo bottles, disposable diapers (unused, please!), potato chip bags

PREPARATION

Arrange a massive "dump" of the items you have collected, approximately 50 feet from the starting line. Intermingle the recyclables with the nonrecyclables.

FORMATION

Divide your group into relay teams of 6 to 8 players each. Line up the teams relay style behind the starting line.

TO PLAY

Give the first "Recycling Ranger" for each team a recycling bin. On "Go" they are to slide the bin to the dump and retrieve 3 recyclable items, then return to their starting point. After unloading the bin onto a pile behind their team, the next person in line slides the bin back to the dump to grab more recyclables. When all the team members have had a turn, the leader checks their recycling pile to verify that everything they retrieved is, in fact, recyclable. The team with the most rescued recyclables wins!

Place	Indoors/Outdoors
Players	12 or More
Time	5 Minutes
Energy	Maximum

Spike 'n Strut

Try this one after a brown bag lunch: recycling at its funniest!

EQUIPMENT

- A paper lunch bag for each player
- An end zone monitor for each team

FORMATION

Relay teams of 6 to 10 players each are needed.

TO PLAY

Each squad (relay team) is lined up relay style on one end zone. On the kickoff signal (GO!), the first running back races down the field to the opposite end zone, paper bag "football" in hand. Upon reaching his goal line, the player blows up the paper bag, does a 5 second victory dance, pops the bag, and spikes it to the ground. (We recognize that individual styles may differ, so it's OK to spike the bag and then do the dance!) When the end zone monitor indicates to the player that he has spiked 'n strutted for the 5 seconds, he races back to his team to touch off the next runner. The first team to finish comes in first. The real winners are those who have been spectating the end zone antics!

Jump Rope Relay

Place	Indoors/Outdoors
Players	12 or More
Time	5 Minutes
Energy	Maximum

This game keeps everyone on their toes!

EQUIPMENT

- A jump rope for each team
- A large, smooth playing surface

FORMATION

Even teams of 6 to 10 players, lined up relay style behind an end line.

TO PLAY

Give the first person on each team a jump rope. At the "Go!" signal, they each run to the designated end line, where they jump rope 10 times. Keeping the rope with them, they race back to their team, and hand one end of the rope to the next person in line. At this point, the rest of the team must be alert, and quick to jump! With the jump rope extended between them, the first two teammates should run on either side of their team's line, holding the rope low enough that each person in turn can jump over it. When the pair reaches the end of the line, the first person becomes the last person in line. The second person takes the rope, and races across the playing area to take a turn jumping rope at the designated end line. Then he hands one end of the rope to the next person in line, and they continue the jumping sequence with the rest of their team. And so the race rages, until the team is back in their original order.

Place	Indoors
Players	12 or More
Time	5 Minutes
Energy	Moderate

Balloon Blow Up

This relay is a good lead-in for other games that require balloons. (It gets the group warmed up, and *saves you from having to blow up balloons in advance!)*

EQUIPMENT

- A balloon for each person, plus some extras in case of defects or accidents

FORMATION

Teams of 6 to 10 players each are needed for this game. Each team should assemble together at an end line.

TO PLAY

Place uninflated balloons across from each team at an opposite end line, approximately 50 feet away. In turn, each team member races up, grabs one balloon, and races back to their team. Once there, inflating and tying the balloons may be done cooperatively, but the race doesn't end until every team member has an inflated, tied balloon lifted high above their heads. (When you give directions for this game, be sure to show your group an example of how big the blown-up balloons should be.) Now that everyone has a balloon, you're ready to go on to another balloon game like *4-Way Balloon Bust Up,* or one of the following relays.

Duck Waddle Relay

Place	Indoors
Players	12 or More
Time	5 Minutes
Energy	Moderate

Use large-sized balloons to really get your group waddling! An hysterical race to watch!

EQUIPMENT

- An inflated balloon per person
- Two beach towels per team

PREPARATION

Place the beach towels opposite each team at an end line approximately 30 feet from the starting line. Arrange towels so they form a circular "nest" to contain the "eggs."

FORMATION

Relay teams of 6 to 8 players each line up relay style behind an end line.

TO PLAY

The first person on each team places his balloon between his legs, just above his knees, sticks his thumbs in his arm pits, and waddles across the playing field. (If the balloon should fall, the player squats down, and tries to grab it with his knees.) When he gets to his team's "nest," he "lays" his "egg" there, and runs back to tap off the next "duck" in line. The race continues until each "duck" has laid his "egg" and rejoined the flock.

Place	Indoors
Players	12 or More
Time	5 Minutes
Energy	Maximum

Balloon Batting Relay

Sometimes balloons seem to have minds of their own. This game will prove it! Try this relay as a lead up to Balloon Batting Battle.

EQUIPMENT

- An inflated balloon per team (with a few extras on hand)
- Cheap paper dinner plates, enough for each person to have 2 or 3, since they're so flimsy

FORMATION

Line your group up relay style, with 6 to 10 players per team. Set up a turning point or end line approximately 50 feet away.

TO PLAY

Players from each team take turns batting the balloon to the end line and back. They may run or walk, whatever works for them, but they must *bat* (not carry or cradle) the balloon with their plates.

If a balloon falls to the floor, the player may simply bat it back up into the air.

First team to have all its players successfully bat the balloon up and back wins.

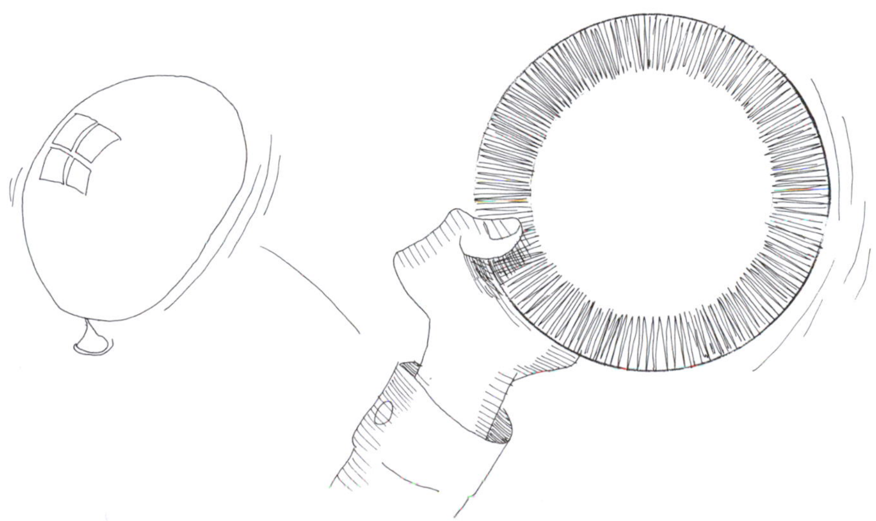

Balloon Sweep Relay

Place	Indoors
Players	12 or More
Time	5 Minutes
Energy	Maximum

Better have a few extra balloons inflated and ready to see action in this race! (If only kids would be so anxious to take a turn with the broom at home!)

EQUIPMENT

- Inflated balloons, one per team, plus some extras
- One broom per team

FORMATION

Assemble teams relay style, with end line approximately 50 feet away. Or, for more confusion (I mean, excitement), arrange four teams in a square, around a central turning prop. (See *Potato Pass,* page 125, for more details.)

TO PLAY

The first player on each team is given a balloon and a broom. On "Go!" each first player sets the balloon on the floor, and sweeps it to the turning point, around it, and back again to his line. Then the next player takes the broom, and continues the balloon sweeping process, and so on, until everyone has had a turn.

If you have enough people to play in the square formation, the player who is sweeping the balloon returns to the **end** of the line, and hands the broom to the second to the last person in line, who bats the balloon gently, and passes the broom on to the next person in line, and so on, until it reaches the front of the line. Then, that person sweeps the balloon out to the turning point, around it, and back to the end of the line. Here the swat-and-pass-the-broom process continues until it reaches the front of the line. Play continues until the team is in its original order.

Place	Indoors
Players	28 to 60
Time	5 Minutes
Energy	Maximum

Potato Pass

Many relays can be done in this square formation. It adds excitement, and keeps everyone on each team involved throughout the race. But, make sure everyone clearly understands which direction they are to run around the central turning point: we want to run into people socially, not physically!

EQUIPMENT

- A central turning point, such as a trash can, or chair
- A chair for each person to sit on
- One raw potato per team

FORMATION

Divide your group into four teams. Give each player a chair, and have each team line up parallel to one of the four walls of the room, facing the center of the room. Make sure the corners of the square are open, allowing room between the ends of the lines. Place the turning point in the center of the group, equidistant from each team.

TO PLAY

The left-most person on each team is given a potato. On "Go!" each of these people race to the central turning point, and run around it clockwise (so their right shoulders are next to it). Then, they race back to the opposite end of their team's line. While they have been racing around, the rest of the team has each slid one chair to the left, filling in the vacant chair on the left, and leaving an empty one on the right end of their line. The returning runner sits in the vacant seat, and hands the potato to the next person, who passes it on to the next, and so on until the potato reaches the person sitting in the left-most chair. When she receives it, she stands up, and races off around the left side of the central turning point, and returns to the now empty chair on the right end of her team's line. The potato is again passed person to person up the line, to the next eagerly awaiting racer. And so the race continues until the team has returned to its original order, and the potato has been returned to the original racer, who is sitting in his original position.

Almost anything can be used to pass in this game. If you can play outdoors, a water balloon or a large ice cube can make for a challenging, fun event!

Hoop Hop Relay

Place	Indoors/Outdoors
Players	16 or More
Time	5 Minutes
Energy	Maximum

This is another relay that keeps the whole team involved the whole time!

EQUIPMENT

- A Hula-Hoop™ for each team

FORMATION

Each relay team of 8 to 12 players stands in a circle, far enough apart to just touch fingertips. Make sure each team has an equal number of players.

TO PLAY

The leader gives one person from each team a Hula-Hoop.™ This person will be the first to run. On the "Go!" command, the runner hands the Hula-Hoop™ to the person to her right. He then extends it to the person to his right, and the two of them hold it while the runner hops through the hoop, jumping out of the circle. Once the runner is safely through, the person holding the right side of the Hula-Hoop™ takes it and extends it to the person to her right. The runner then hops back through the hoop, to the inside of the circle, and waits until the Hula-Hoop™ is positioned between the next two players, so she can continue weaving her way around the circle. Once she returns to her original position, the runner takes the Hula-Hoop,™ and holds it with the person to her right. The person to her left becomes the next runner, and he proceeds hopping through the hoop as it is passed along. The race continues until everyone has had a turn being the runner, and the Hula-Hoop™ is back in the hands of the original runner.

Place	Indoors
Players	12 or More
Time	5 Minutes
Energy	Moderate

Antarctic Adventure

An obstacle course in disguise, this game is well-suited for groups with good imaginations who enjoy wacky races.

EQUIPMENT

- Large cardboard box per team (apple or banana sized ones)
- 2 sections of newspaper per team, plus extras on hand
- Cone or similar object to act as the South Pole
- Masking tape

FORMATION

Each team of 6 to 8 players lines up in single file. Place teams equidistant from "Antarctica," either in a semicircle, or one team at each compass point, at a distance of about 60 feet from the pole. A cardboard box should be placed in front of each team. About 20 feet closer to the Pole, set two sections of newspaper down, in front of each team. At another 20 feet closer to the Pole, lay a strip of masking tape.

TO PLAY

When the "Captain" gives the command to go, the first explorer from each team hops into his cardboard boat, and creatively propels himself with his arms to the coast of Antarctica. There, he leaves his boat, and dons his cross-country skis (a.k.a. the newspaper). He slides his way to the polar cap, as marked by the masking tape. Here he sheds his skis, and assumes the penguin position: ankles together, toes apart, arms straight down, with hands held out. Our explorer must penguin walk around the Pole, and back to his skis. He then skis back to his awaiting boat. Leaving the skis for the next person from his group, he boats back to his team, to the next anxious explorer. And so goes the exploration of Antarctica!

The Space Shuttle Shuffle

Place	Indoors/Outdoors
Players	16 or More
Time	5 Minutes
Energy	Maximum

This is a "fun any time, any place" kind of a relay, because it requires no props. The astronaut in all of us comes through in this one. For a special effect sometime, decorate beach balls with glow-in-the-dark paint to serve as space stations. Give each team a glo-stick to light their way and to pass on to the next racer. Combine this game with an Alien Assault Flashlight Tag game, and you've got a Space Party! (Have plenty of Moon Pies on hand for refreshments!)

EQUIPMENT

- None (glow-in-the-dark beach ball and/or glo-stick optional)

FORMATION

Line up even teams relay style. Mark an end line approximately 30 feet away.

TO PLAY

On "Go," the first player from each team rockets off into outer space, in the direction of the space station (the end line opposite their team). They return to their teams, grab the hand of the next astronaut in line, and race back to the space station. The original astronaut is left there to begin doing whatever astronauts do at space stations. The second player runs back to the team, grabs the next one in line, and together they blast off for the final frontier. Once at the space station, the second astronaut is left to man the operations, while the first astronaut is shuttled back to earth. And so the race through space goes, with a continual changing of space station astronauts, until all players (except the last one) have spent some time alone at the space station. The last astronaut in line is a fine shuttle pilot, and she makes a solo return trip for our remaining space station attendant.

Place	Indoors/Outdoors
Players	12 or More
Time	5 Minutes
Energy	Maximum

Whisper Down The Raceway

A variation of Whisper Down the Alley, this game has an active twist. Players still pass a secret message, but the next player is standing across the room!

EQUIPMENT

- Slips of paper with secret messages written on them

FORMATION

The group is divided into equal teams, with half of the members from each team lined up across the room, at a distance of approximately 30 feet.

TO PLAY

The first person on each team is given a written message. (Make it something nonsensical, like, "Lily Logan likes to lick lollipops while her pet walrus Wilbur watches wrestling on TV.") They read the message silently, crumple up the paper, and throw it down before racing off to tell the next player what was written. Accuracy is more important than speed, but all players should run. When the last player has run the raceway, he whispers the message to the leader. The team with the most accurate rendition of the original wins!

Spear The Sweets

Place	Indoors/Outdoors
Players	12 or More
Time	5 Minutes
Energy	Moderate

It's amazing how quickly your program turns into a party, just by bringing out a bowl of candy!

EQUIPMENT

- Toothpick for each player
- Small plastic bowl for each team
- Semihard candies, enough for each team member, plus extras (jelly beans or Raisinets® work well)

FORMATION

Divide your group into equal teams, and have them line up relay style. Place a bowl of candy opposite each team, at a distance of 50 feet.

TO PLAY

Give each player a toothpick to hold. On "Go," the first person races up to the bowl, and spears a sweet with her toothpick. She then races back to her team and carefully feeds it to the next person in line. This is their signal to take a turn spearing a sweet. The first team finished gets the extra candy!

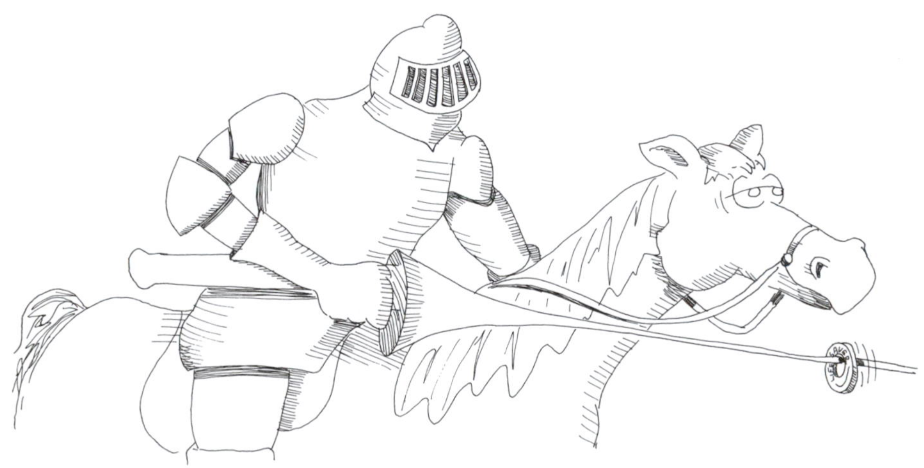

Place	Indoors/Outdoors
Players	12 or More
Time	5 Minutes
Energy	Maximum

Elastic Band Relay

Now here's a prop that is so much fun to use, you'll be thinking up other activities just to use your elastic bands more!

EQUIPMENT

- One elastic band per team (to make elastic band, take one yard of 1/2 inch elastic, overlap the ends one inch, and stitch securely)

FORMATION

Divide your group into even teams, and line them up relay style.

TO PLAY

Place an elastic band opposite each team, at a distance of 50 feet. On "Go," the first player races to the elastic band, picks it up over his head, and pushes it down over his body. After he steps out of it, he leaves the elastic band there, and runs back to tag off the next player.

For a more comical event, have your teams pair up, and watch the antics as each couple tries to maneuver the elastic band down and around the two of them!

Inheritance

Place	Indoors/Outdoors
Players	16 or More
Time	5 Minutes
Energy	Maximum

The pace of this game slows as it goes on, but the hilarity increases dramatically!

EQUIPMENT

- A card table or desk for each team
- Each team needs a prop for each person, and each team should have the same props. For example, each team of eight should have a pair of rubber gloves, a broom, a roll of toilet paper, a section of newspaper, a box of cereal, a folding chair, a hat, and an inflated balloon. (This list is an example. Use props that are readily available to you, and appropriate for your group.)

FORMATION

Line even teams up relay style, with the tables full of props opposite each team, at a distance of 30 feet.

TO PLAY

On "Go," the first player from each team runs across the playing field to the table of props, and selects one (*any* one). She returns to the line with her selected prop, and passes it on to the next player in line. This player keeps a hold of the first prop, and races up to the table to select a second prop. He then returns to the line, and passes on both pieces. And so the race continues, with each successive person inheriting yet another priceless heirloom. Please note: no one may help with the exchange of the props. Each new runner must collect the items from the previous by himself. If at any time a prop drops to the floor, a referee must return it to the table, and the group must make another trip to get it (while lugging along everything else, as well!).

Place	Indoors/Outdoors
Players	20 or More
Time	10 to 15 Minutes
Energy	Moderate

Ridiculous Request Relay

Here's a ridiculously funny relay you can tailor to your group. It's a madcap adventure sure to please any fun-loving group!

EQUIPMENT

- Each team will need at least one request slip per person, plus appropriate props to complete the task. Each team should have the same requests written on their slips, though they will be selected in differing orders.
- A central table to hold props and request slips
- A "baton" to be passed between players (rubber spatulas, paper towel rolls, or rolled and taped newspapers do fine)
- A chair for each player, if possible

FORMATION

Divide your group into even teams of 10 or more players, with a maximum of 4 teams. Assemble the teams so the entire group makes a square approximately 30 feet by 30 feet, with each side of the square being a different team. If sufficient numbers of chairs are available, have each person sit in a chair . The table of props and request slips should be in the center of the square.

TO PLAY

Hand the left-most person on each team a "baton." On the "Go!" signal, that person from each team runs up to the table, sets down her baton, and selects a request slip. (These slips may be in a bag, or folded in half, and taped to the edge of the table facing their team.) Upon reading the slip, she must perform the prescribed task, take back the baton from the table, and return to the opposite end of her team's line. While the first player has been performing her ridiculous request, the rest of her team has each shifted one seat to the left, making a vacant seat available at the right end of the line. When the first runner returns to the last seat in line, she passes the baton to the person to her immediate left, who continues to pass it person to person on up the line, until the new left-most person has the baton. As soon as he receives it, he races up to the table to perform his ridiculous request. And so the game goes, until all the slips are used up, or until the first person is back in her original position, with baton in hand.

EXAMPLES OF RIDICULOUS REQUESTS:

- Run back to your team, and lead them in doing 10 jumping jacks. Have everyone count LOUDLY!
- Take a piece of bubble gum from the table. Chew it, and blow a bubble for the referee at the table.
- Shake hands with all the seated players of a different team.
- Sit under this table and bark like a dog 5 times.
- Put your thumbs in your armpits, and crow "Cock-a-doodle-doo!" as loudly as you can.
- Take a balloon (uninflated) from the table. Blow it up and tie it. Run back to your team, grab a helper by the hand and to return to the table with him/her. Have your helper stomp the balloon to burst it.
- Get a helper from your team, and return to the table. Take the elastic band from the table, and slip it over both your heads, and down your bodies. Return elastic band to the table.
- Take a Hershey's® kiss from the table. Go to a cute guy/girl, and ask them as LOUDLY as you can, "WOULD YOU LIKE A KISS?" Give them one.
- Run around the back of your team, and pat each person on the back.
- Get a helper from your team, and return to the table. Take a balloon, blow it up and tie it. Then hold the balloon between the two of you, and squeeze together to pop it (NO HANDS ALLOWED!)

Place	Indoors
Players	12 or More
Time	5 Minutes
Energy	Moderate

Spelling Relay

Even if you never were much of a speller, you'll enjoy this relay!

EQUIPMENT

- A small bowl per team
- 6-10 folded slips of paper with spelling words on them. Each team should have identical lists.
- Small paper plates, or note cards with letters of the alphabet written on them, enough for each team to spell each word

FORMATION

Divide your group into even teams of 6 to 8 each, and have them line up relay style behind a starting line. Across from each team, at a distance of 30 to 50 feet, place the paper plates and bowls of spelling words.

TO PLAY

The first two players from each team race across the playing area, and select a word from the bowl. Using the lettered paper plates, they spell out the word, leaving it on the floor behind the bowl. They return to their team, and touch off the next two players in line, who select a new word to spell out. The game continues until all the words are spelled out.

Select words appropriate to your program theme, or to your group. Be sure you have enough paper plates lettered for each team to spell out each word—plus a few extra letters to keep it interesting for the last set of runners!

Wobble Ball Relay

Place	Indoors/Outdoors
Players	20 or More
Time	5 Minutes
Energy	Maximum

Speed and accuracy are critical for success in this relay—but when you're trying to toss a lopsided object, there's no telling what might happen!

EQUIPMENT

- A 9" balloon, inflated, with small rubber ball inside, per team

FORMATION

Divide your group into teams of 10 to 16 each. Have each team split in half, with both halves lined up single file, relay style, at a distance of 15 to 20 feet from each other, with the first players facing each other.

TO PLAY

The directions are quite simple: the first person in line tosses the balloon to the first person on the other half of their team's line. After one tosses the balloon, she runs to the back of the opposite line. The balloon and players move back and forth, until the players and the balloon are in their original position. Sounds simple enough, but this becomes a wacky game of toss since the balloon is weighted, and may not go where you aimed it! Frivolity reigns in this game!

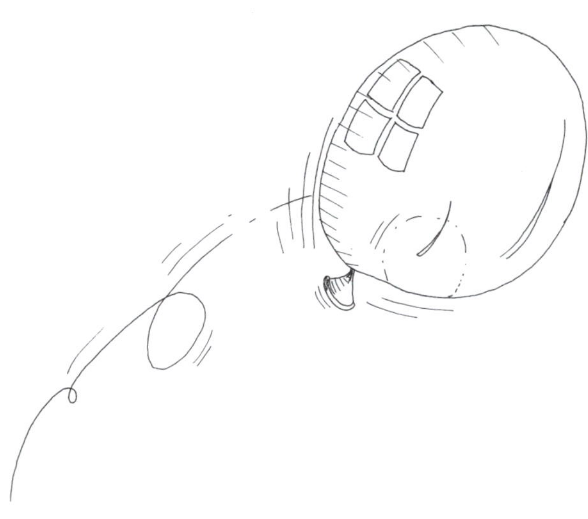

Place	Indoors/Outdoors
Players	12 or More
Time	5 Minutes
Energy	Moderate

Motley Medley

The nonskilled legs of this relay help to even out the teams, and make for some hilarious spectating!

EQUIPMENT

- One jump rope per team
- A basketball per team
- One bandana per team
- 4 brooms and 8 chairs, or other props to be used as hurdles
- 4 or more Hula-Hoops™
- Paper towel tubes or other cylinders to use as batons for each team

FORMATION

Divide your group into teams of 6 each. Have a member from each team station themselves at one of six starting positions, which are spaced 30 to 50 feet apart, in a large circle. Assemble the necessary props at each of the stations or running areas.

TO PLAY

Hand the first runner from each team a baton, which will be passed from player to player as the race progresses. On "Go," the first racer jumps rope to the next station, and hands off the baton to their teammate. That player walks backward to the next station, holding onto his ankles tightly with both hands. At Station 3, the next racer places a basketball between his legs, and waddles off to the next station, baton in hand. After she receives the baton, the next player (whose ankles are tied together with a bandana) springs her way to her awaiting teammate. Racer number 5 performs the low hurdles. But instead of going *over* the brooms which are supported by the chairs, he goes *under* them. The anchor runner races back to the starting line, but must jump with both feet into the Hula-Hoops™ which are staggered across the racing field.

Pepsi® Pass

Place	Indoors/Outdoors
Players	16 or More
Time	5 Minutes
Energy	Moderate

File this game in the back of your mind. It's a great "impromptu game time" game!

EQUIPMENT

- A 1- or 2-liter empty soda bottle per team

FORMATION

Divide your group into teams of 8 to 20. For smaller teams, have them stand relay style, an arm's distance behind the player in front of them. If you are playing with large teams, ask them to stand in a circle, with hands on the shoulders of the players on either side of them.

TO PLAY

Play begins with the empty soda bottles standing on the floor in front of the first player on each team. On "Go," that player picks up the bottle and places it between his legs, above his knees. He then turns to the next player in line, who grabs the bottle with her legs, turns and passes it on to the next player. Once the bottle is in play, no one may touch the bottle with his hands. If the bottle falls, only feet and legs may be used to retrieve it.

Place	Indoors
Players	16 or More
Time	5 Minutes
Energy	Minimal

Chicken In Every Pot

If you've got a gregarious group, this may be the only time some of them are silent! Change the shape of your object to match your theme or season.

EQUIPMENT

- A drinking straw per person, plus extras
- Two paper bowls per team
- A cutout paper chicken, 3" to 4" in size, per team

FORMATION

Divide your group into teams of 8 to 12 players each. Have them stand relay style, with the first person in line holding a bowl with the chicken in it. The last person in each line should have an empty paper bowl. All players should have a straw in their hands.

TO PLAY

On the "Go!" command, the first player puts one end of the straw in her mouth, and the other on the paper chicken. By inhaling, she should remove the chicken from the bowl, and slowly turn toward the next player in line. That player puts one end of his straw in his mouth, and sucks the chicken off the other player's straw, and onto his. Thus the chicken gets passed from person to person, down the line, until it makes it to its final resting place: the "pot" at the other end of the line. If the chicken should "take flight" at any point along its journey, the player who dropped it must retrieve it by using her straw only.

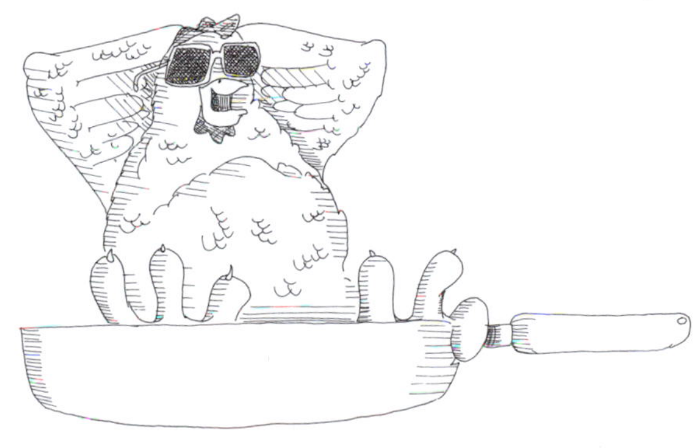

52 Card Pick Up

Place	Indoors
Players	12 or More
Time	5 Minutes
Energy	Maximum

This game is as much fun to set up as it is to play!

EQUIPMENT

- A deck of playing cards, or more, so each team has an entire suit of cards

FORMATION

Break your group into teams of 6 to 13 players. Have them line up relay style, approximately 30 to 50 feet from the pile of scattered playing cards.

TO PLAY

The object of this race is to gather a complete suit of playing cards. One team should be assigned to retrieve the hearts, another the diamonds, another the spades, and the last, clubs. If more than four teams are playing, use additional decks of cards with different print on the back, if possible. In turn, the teammates race to the pile of cards, and rummage through them trying to locate the next needed card in their assigned suit. The first player should bring back the Ace, the second runner should bring back the number 2 card in their suit, the third the number 3 card, and so on. Runners need to continue taking turns retrieving cards until all 13 cards in their suit have been gathered and laid out in a row.

Place	Indoors
Players	16 or More
Time	5 Minutes
Energy	Moderate

Bandana Balance

A bandana doesn't have to be balanced on your head the way a book does, but racing with a bandana on your head isn't as easy as it sounds!

EQUIPMENT

- One bandana per team

FORMATION

Assemble evenly divided teams of 8 to 12, relay style, behind an end line. Designate a turning point about 30 feet away.

TO PLAY

Give the first player on each team a bandana. Without folding it or tying it in any way, have each of them place the open bandana on the top of their head. On "Go," they race to the turning point and back to their team, without touching the bandana! If the bandana does fall off a racer's head, she must stop, touch the bandana to the floor, then place it back on her head and continue back to her team. Here she hands off the bandana to the next player in line—head to head—without using hands. This is a funny game to watch—and play!

Swallowing Goldfish

Place	Indoors/Outdoors
Players	16 or More
Time	10 to 15 Minutes
Energy	Moderate

Thanks to Pepperidge Farms,® we no longer have to use the live ones for this game!

EQUIPMENT

- Goldfish crackers
- Plastic spoon per player
- Dish or cup per team
- A chair for each player

FORMATION

Divide your group into even teams of 8 to 12. Have teams sit in chairs that have been arranged in a square, with each team sitting on one side of the square. The last chair on the right of each side should be moved in front of the next teammate's chair, so these two players face each other. Hand each player a clean spoon, and give the player on the far left end of each team a bowl full of goldfish.

TO PLAY

On the "Go!" command, the first player scoops a spoonful of goldfish out of the bowl, and slides them into the spoon of the next player. The goldfish continue player to player, spoon to spoon, until they reach the last player in line. When she receives the goldfish, she begins tossing them one at a time into the awaiting mouth of the teammate who is facing her. (He should be positioned about 3 feet in front of her.) As soon as he successfully swallows one goldfish, that player stands up and races to the front of the line, and takes the chair and cup of goldfish from the first person. Simultaneously, all the other team members shift one chair, so the person who just threw the goldfish will now have the opportunity to eat one. The passing of the goldfish resumes, and play continues until each player has swallowed a goldfish, and the team is in its original position.

Place	Indoors/Outdoors
Players	16 or More
Time	5 Minutes
Energy	Maximum

Licorice Lunacy Race

Once you've got the basic race down, add as much lunacy to it as your laughter muscles can handle!

EQUIPMENT

- Shoestring licorice, enough for each couple to have a piece
- Two bandanas per team
- A cone or turning marker per team

FORMATION

Have your group couple up, and organize the couples into even teams. Line up the couples in teams behind an end line. Place a turning marker opposite each team, at a distance of 40 to 50 feet.

TO PLAY

Blindfold the first couple on each team, and have them put their hands behind their backs. Place the ends of one licorice strand in their mouths. On "Go," the first couples eat their way to the center of the licorice shoestring. When they meet in the middle, they may remove their blindfolds, and the girls jumps onto their partners' backs. Together, they go racing across the field, to the cone. There they must circle the cone three times before returning to touch off the next couple.

VARIATION

When the couple reaches the turning point, have an elastic band waiting for them to slip over their heads and work down their bodies. Once this task is completed, they return to their team.

Bombs Away!

Place	Indoors
Players	16 or More
Time	5 Minutes
Energy	Moderate

The more you laugh, the messier you get!

EQUIPMENT

- Large bowl of seedless grapes, per team
- Bowl of whipped cream, per team
- Napkins or paper towels for floor and people cleanup
- A helper at each of the grape bowls

FORMATION

Divide your group into even teams made up of couples. Have the teams line up relay style in couples. Across from each team, at a distance of 30 feet or so, place the bowls of grapes and whipped cream.

TO PLAY

The first couple from each team holds hands, and races to the bowls of food. There they lie down head to head. The helper there assists the girl in putting both bowls on her abdomen. The girl takes one grape, dips it in the whipped cream, and attempts to drop it into the mouth of her partner. With both partners still lying head to head, she continues in this feeding effort until she succeeds. Once she does, the helper moves both bowls to the guy's abdomen, and he takes a turn feeding his partner. Once both players have fed and been fed, they bounce back to their feet, join (slippery!) hands, and race back to the next anxiously awaiting couple!

Place	Indoors/Outdoors
Players	20 or More
Time	5 Minutes or Less
Energy	Moderate

Raisinet® Racing

Most any smooth rolling food could be substituted for the Raisinets.® If your kids enjoy this game, play it at suppertime. What a great way to get them to eat their vegetables!

EQUIPMENT

- Two paper towel tubes per team (wrapping paper tubes would also work well)
- Paper cup full of Raisinets® per team

FORMATION

Divide your group into even teams of 10 to 16 each. Have them line up relay style, then pull every other one out slightly to one side. Give the first person on each half-line of the team a paper towel tube. Set the cups of Raisinets® on the floor in front to the teams.

TO PLAY

The object of this race is to get a Raisinet® to roll through the tubes (which are being passed down the line) to the open mouth of the last player in line. Once he gets a Raisinet® in his mouth, he takes the two tubes with him as he races back to the front of the line, to start another Raisinet® on its way. If a Raisinet® should fall on the floor en route, it is discarded. The tubes are returned to the front of the line where they can begin transporting another sweet morsel. The first team to successfully feed each player, and return to its original starting lineup wins!

Face To Face

Place	Indoors
Players	20 or More
Time	5 Minutes
Energy	Moderate

This is a funny game to watch—whether your face is smeared into a balloon or not!

EQUIPMENT

- 10-inch balloons, enough for each couple to have one, plus extras
- Cones to mark end line

FORMATION

Have your group members find a partner, then group partners together to form even teams. Line the teams up in their couples, and give each couple an uninflated balloon. Set cones up about 40 feet away.

TO PLAY

On "Go," the first couple from each team blows up their balloon, ties it, and places it between their faces. (Yep, that's what I said!) With the balloon held in this position, they run to the end line. Here, they let the balloon drop slightly, catching it between their torsos. Once it is in place, they press their bodies together, popping the balloon without using their hands. Whew! That all done, they race back to their team to tag off the next eager couple!

CHAPTER 8

Quiet Games

Quiet games. A hush falls over the crowd. A gentle wind lightly rustles the leaves. The soothing babble of a nearby brook beckons, "Be still. Be at peace."

O.K. So I made that up. Most of us won't find ourselves leading groups in such tranquil settings. And even if we did, it would be drown out by the playful screams and squeals of rock skippers and tree climbers!

Still and all, there is a place for quiet activities in your program. They serve as a contrast to the high speed pace of life, provide a breather after a highly active game, and make an effective closing activity for your program. Recall the programming wave analogy from Chapter 3. Culminating your program with a calming, closing activity eases the participant back onto the shore of life after your program: it prevents participants from being body slammed onto the beach of everyday life!

Quiet games need not be silent, or still, or boring. They require minimal physical effort, but produce maximum enjoyment. Review the following selections, and give some a try!

Tanks

Place	Indoors/Outdoors
Players	12 to 24
Time	10 to 15 Minutes
Energy	Minimal

Tanks is a game of combat—without the contact or violence!

EQUIPMENT

- Fire Power cards for each player, plus several extras (directions below)

PREPARATION

Make Fire Power cards by cutting scrap paper into approximately 4" x 6" pieces. On each card, write a number between 50 and 150. Some of the cards may have the same number on them. Fold cards in half to conceal number.

TO PLAY

Divide your group in half, and have the two teams line up opposite each other, about 15 feet apart. The leader invites the first tank in line on team A to challenge any tank on the opposing team. Both tanks rumble to the center, and hand their Fire Power card to the leader. The leader declares the tank with the higher fire power the winner of this skirmish. The winning tank returns to its base, Fire Power card in hand. The defeated tank limps off to the sidelines, having surrendered his Fire Power card to the leader. If both tanks have the same fire power, they each select another tank to back them up. The backup tank with the highest fire power saves her tank mate, and sends both of the opposing tanks to the tank heap. Play continues until one team is completely annihilated. For this game to be effective, no one should show *any* other player their fire power. Shuffle cards and redistribute them between rounds.

Singing

What! Sing?! ME??!!

Before you talk yourself out of leading your group in some songs, let's think about it. You may not have a concert quality voice. Most of us don't. But many people derive much pleasure from singing, and all they need is someone to suggest it, and that gets the singing started.

The basics of song leading are much the same as leading other recreation activities. As a leader, you should be familiar with what you are going to lead (like knowing the words and the tune for the song!). You should lead enthusiastically, and be sensitive to how your group is responding. Once the group has been started, you might find a group member who is particularly skilled at song leading, who may enjoy leading the singing herself. Take advantage of such skills found within your group, and allow group members to develop their leadership skills as well.

To introduce a song to the group, tell the title, and something about the song. If the tune is a familiar one, tell them so. Sing the song through once for them, then tell them the words clearly and slowly. If you prefer, have the words written on a sheet of paper, and posted for all to see. Sing the song through with them, prompting them with the next line of words as you go. Clear up any confusion, then take it again from the top!

"Brussels Sprouts And Peanut Butter" Song

Tune: Three Blind Mice

Words:
Brussels sprouts. Brussels sprouts.
With peanut butter. With peanut butter.
Brussels sprouts with peanut butter
Go together like no other.
Go ahead and ask your Mother, for
Brussels sprouts!

More Words:
Brush your teeth. Brush your teeth.
With peanut butter. With peanut butter.
Brush your teeth with peanut butter,
They stick together like no other.
Try it out on your kid brother, then
Brush your teeth!

"Take Me Out To The Mall, Mom" Song

Tune: Take Me Out to the Ball Game

Words:
Take me out to the mall, Mom!
Take me out to the shops.
Buy me the latest accessories.
I've got to keep up with the others I see.
I want more, more, more of what *they've* got:
New things are better, and how!
So come on, Mom, hurry, let's go.
There's a sale on now!

Personalities

Place	Indoors
Players	8 to 12
Time	20 to 30 Minutes
Energy	Minimal

I learned this game around a campfire, at the beginning of a several week backpacking trip with a group of fellow students. We didn't know each other well when we started, but we did by the end of the trip! And the more we played this game, the better we got to know each other.

EQUIPMENT

- Scrap paper and pencil for the leader

TO PLAY

Have your group sit in a circle. Give them a topic, such as Favorite Animal, but warn them *not* to tell any other players what they have chosen. With pencil and paper in hand, walk around to each person, and have them whisper in your ear what they have chosen. If they have chosen an animal which someone else already selected, have them chose another one. Keep a list of all the animals given to you, though not necessarily in the order they were given. When each person has told you their animal, divide the group into 3 teams, and read the list. Remind the players not to tell anyone which animal is theirs! After you have read the list, the first team confers, and asks someone from another team if a particular animal is theirs. If it is, that person joins the guessing team, and the team gets another turn. If the team guesses incorrectly, the play goes on to the next team. A team may guess a previously guessed player, but ONLY after they have guessed someone new.

There is a lot of player movement between teams, as they get "guessed away" to other teams. The suspense of revealing the final unknown players often brings a climax to the game. In all, Personalities does reveal some of our personalities to one another. It is especially effective to play with a group that has been together for a while, such as with a youth group, or at on a scout camping trip, or even with extended family while the Thanksgiving turkey settles.

VARIATIONS

This game may be played for several rounds at a session. Get suggestions for categories from the participants. Other topics could include:

- Favorite food
- Cars
- Cartoon character you identify with
- Your favorite athlete
- Historical figure you really admire

Place	Indoors
Players	Any Number
Time	5 Minutes
Energy	Minimal

Ridiculous Responses

Ask a silly question, you get a RIDICULOUS Response! This ludicrous exercise is a laugh a minute. Try it and see!

EQUIPMENT

- Paper and pencil for each person
- Two bags, boxes, or hats to hold responses

FORMATION

Random gathering of players.

TO PLAY

Give each person a pencil and a sheet of paper. On the top of the page, each person should write a question beginning with the phrase, "What would you do if..." Once each has written her question, she should rip the paper in half, and deposit the question sheet into one of the bags. On the remainder of the paper slips, ask participants to answer their question, beginning with the phrase, "I would..." These responses should be placed into the second bag. Let everyone select a slip of paper from each bag, and read their question and its "corresponding" answer. Some RIDICULOUS and hilarious responses may result!

For a variation, have questions begin with "Why..." and have answers begin with "Because..."

State Stars

Place	Indoors
Players	6 to 15
Time	10 to 15 Minutes
Energy	Minimal

Here is a fun mind stretcher (and a good learning tool). Adapt this game to any kind of "fun facts!"

EQUIPMENT

- 50 stars, approximately 4" in size, or 3 x 5 cards with large stars drawn on one side. Label each star with the name of one of the 50 states.
- Masking tape to tack them to the wall
- Answer sheet, if necessary

FORMATION

Have group sit in a circle, semicircle, or rows, so you can easily keep track of whose turn it is.

TO PLAY

Have the first person select a star from the wall, and read aloud the name of the state written on the back. He then has 10 seconds to tell the group the name of its capital. If he correctly names it, he may keep the star. If he is unable to name the capital, the next group member in line may take a shot at it. Whoever correctly names the capital keeps the star. Play continues down the line, until all 50 states have been drawn. The person with the most stars at the end of the game wins!

For a variation, try putting the state's nickname on the back of the card, and have players try to identify the state.

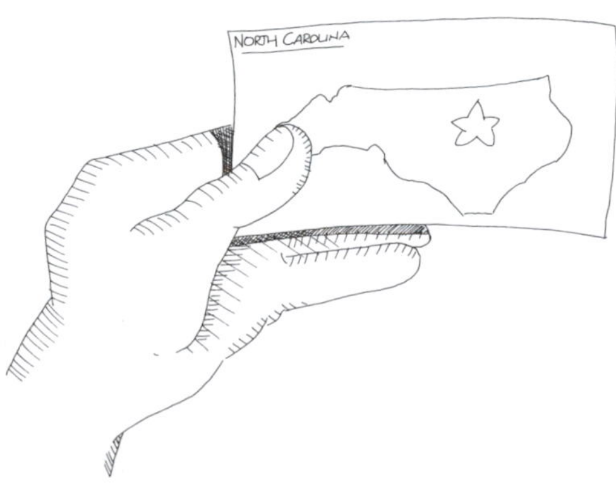

Place	Indoors
Players	Any Number
Time	5 Minutes
Energy	Minimal

Confused Cats

Whether your group is feline friendly or not, they'll enjoy the challenge of trying to identify words containing "cat" from these clues!

EQUIPMENT

- Pencil and prepared sheet for each participant

FORMATION

Randomly seated, or seated at tables.

TO PLAY

Give each person a sheet of paper with these clues on it, and see how many they can identify.

1. A mail-order cat? (Catalogue)
2. A saucy cat? (Catsup)
3. An ancient cemetery cat? (Catacombs)
4. A flying cat? (Catbird)
5. A major mishap cat? (Catastrophe)
6. A group of horned cats? (Cattle)
7. A problem with eyes? (Cataracts)
8. A swimming cat? (Catfish)
9. A many-tailed cat? (Cat-o'-nine-tails)
10. An aromatic cat? (Catnip)
11. A baseball playing cat? (Catcher)
12. An easy to remember phrase cat? (Catchy)
13. A narrow walkway cat? (Catwalk)
14. A make-things-happen-quicker cat? (Catalyst)
15. A sailing cat? (Catamaran)
16. A shooting cat? (Catapult)
17. A tennis racket cat? (Catgut)
18. A diagonal cat? (Catty-cornered)
19. A larva cat? (Caterpillar)
20. A classified cat? (Categorize)

Nutty Questionnaire

Place	Indoors
Players	Any Number
Time	5 Minutes
Energy	Minimal

Here's another mind-stretching exercise to challenge your group.

EQUIPMENT

- Pencil and prepared sheet of paper per participant

FORMATION

Randomly seated, or seated at tables.

TO PLAY

Distribute pencils and prepared sheets to all participants. See how many "nuts" they can identify from the list below.

1. A part of a room nut? (Walnut)
2. A green vegetable nut? (Peanut)
3. What nut is beside the sea? (Beechnut)
4. An uncooked bread nut? (Doughnut)
5. A nut from a dairy product? (Butternut)
6. A nut with a girls' name? (Hazelnut)
7. A storage container nut? (Chestnut)
8. A crunchy cereal? (Grapenuts®)
9. A hot drink? (Cocoanut)
10. A brief, concise statement? (Nutshell)
11. A spicy nut? (Nutmeg)
12. A bird? (Nuthatch)
13. A ballet? (Nutcracker)
14. Craziness? (Nutty)
15. An evergreen nut? (Pine nut)

Place	Indoors
Players	Any Number
Time	10 to 15 Minutes
Energy	Minimal

Toothpick Mind Pricks

Have these games on hand to challenge group members when they arrive at your program early, or leave late, or for any quiet time.

EQUIPMENT

- Box of toothpicks
- Sheets of paper each with a challenge written on it

FORMATION

Randomly arranged, or at a table.

TO PLAY

Hand out prepared sheets and toothpicks, or have them set up at stations around the room. Participants may play individually, or in small groups. (Be ready to give clues if you notice frustration levels rising!)

1. Form nine squares with 24 toothpicks:

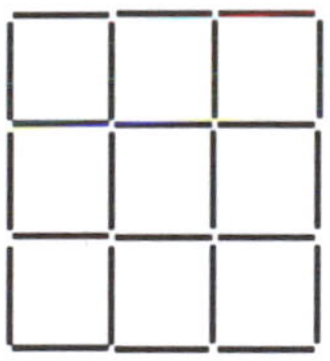

Remove 8 toothpicks and leave two squares.

Solution:

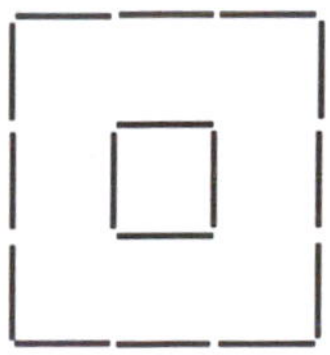

2. With 12 toothpicks, form four squares:

Remove 4 toothpicks, and replace them, leaving three squares.

Solution:

3. With 15 toothpicks, make five squares:

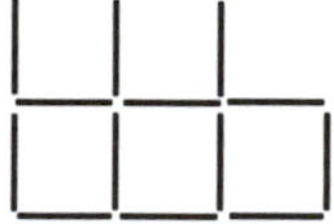

Remove 3 toothpicks, and leave three squares.

Solution:

4. Use six toothpicks to make 11, without breaking any:

Solution: Form the Roman numeral for 11:

5. Use these six toothpicks to show that half of 11 is six: XI

   Solution: Take away bottom half of the numeral, leaving vi. VI

6. Use six toothpicks to make 25:

   Solution: XXV

7. Lay 6 toothpicks in a row, as illustrated:

   Add 5 toothpicks to make 9.

   Solution: NINE

8. Hand a player 9 toothpicks, and ask her to make 10, without breaking any of the toothpicks:

   Solution: TEN

9. Place one end of each of 10 toothpicks in a gum drop, so they stand upright. Challenge someone to arrange the 10 toothpicks in five lines, of 4 toothpicks each:

   Solution: A Star, with a toothpick at each intersection:

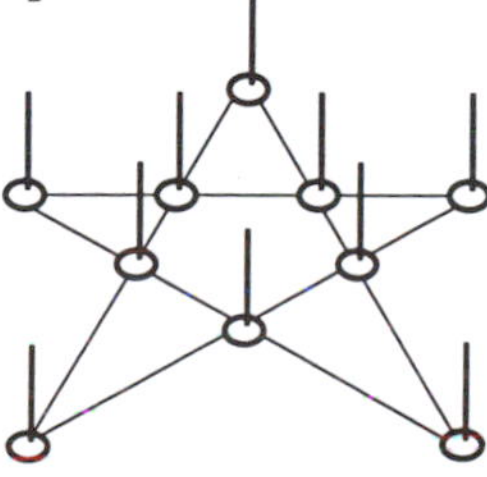

10. Form a large square out of 16 toothpicks. This represents a farmers land. The farmer wants to leave his land to his five sons. The eldest son is to receive the largest share, one corner of the property, which equals one-quarter of the total area. The remaining four sons are to receive equal shares. Mark off the eldest son's portion using four toothpicks. If each of the other brothers is given two toothpicks to mark off their portions, how might they do it so each would receive an equal area of land?

Solution:

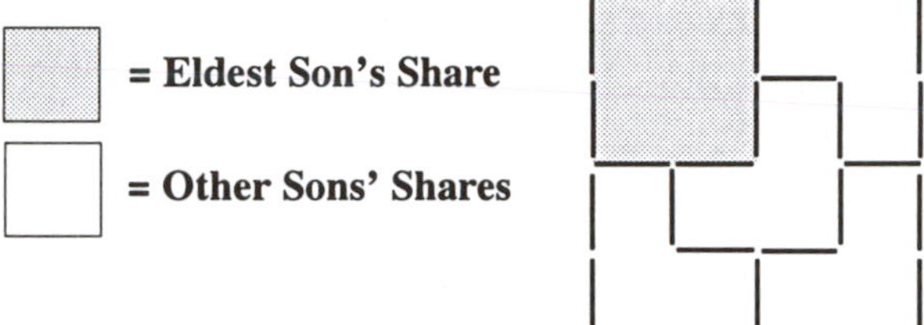

Place	Indoors
Players	8 to 16
Time	10 to 15 Minutes
Energy	Minimal

Airplane Adventure

Ever want to do some world traveling, but never had the finances to do it? Airplane Adventure is just the game for you!

EQUIPMENT

- Large world map taped to the wall
- Little paper airplanes for each person, labeled with their name
- Masking tape
- Colored circle of paper, or other marker to denote take-off point
- A chair
- Blindfold
- Yardstick or string to measure flights

FORMATION

Players may line up behind the "layover" chair, or along sides of pathway. A chair is place 10 to 15 feet away from the wall, facing the map.

TO PLAY

Distribute paper airplanes, with tape "doughnuts" on the back. Give players a few minutes to review the map, noting the location of the take-off point. In turn, blindfold a player, and stand him with his back to the map. He must begin his Airplane Adventure with a "layover" (by walking to and carefully sitting in the chair). He then stands up, walks back to the wall, and places his airplane on the map, as far away from the starting point as possible. If he places his plane in water, it is considered lost at sea. The player whose airplane takes the longest flight from the take-off point wins!

Match 'em

Place	Indoors
Players	10 to 20
Time	20 to 30 Minutes
Energy	Minimal

You may not have a studio audience on hand, but you can sure have a good time playing this take-off on the old TV game show, The Match Game. *If possible, have "valuable" prizes to award, and a humorous emcee to officiate!*

EQUIPMENT

- Pencils and a stack of scrap paper for each player
- Something to act as a scoreboard and marker
- List of questions (see below for examples)

FORMATION

The group should be divided into two teams of 5 to 10 each, and seated at a tables 10 feet apart, opposite each other. The emcee should stand between the two teams' tables, at one end. The captains of each team should stand or sit close to him.

TO PLAY

Alternating between teams, the emcee should read a question from his list. All players on that team write an answer to the question without looking at anyone else's answer. The team's responses are then passed to the emcee, who reads them aloud. For every answer that matches the team captain's, the team is awarded five points. For example, the question might be, "Which team will be the Super Bowl champions next year?" If the team captain writes, "The Steelers," her team will be awarded five points for each team member who also wrote "The Steelers."

Every few rounds, you may want to take a "commercial break" and rotate players to get new team captains. If your group is a large one, you may want to rotate in new players, or let some work up "commercials" to present to the group! And don't forget to let "Bob" tell us about some of those "valuable prizes!"

The game continues through a set number of rounds, or until one team has earned a predetermined number of points.

Some sample questions follow, but be sure you have plenty of group-appropriate ones on hand!

1. Name something yellow.
2. What is your favorite kind of car?
3. What is the best fast food place in town?
4. Name something you would find in the freezer.
5. What country would you most like to visit?
6. If you could have any kind of animal for a pet, what would it be?
7. What is your favorite movie?
8. What is your favorite dessert?
9. If you could meet one movie star, who would it be?
10. If you could play (instantly) any instrument, which would you want to play?

Jeopardy

Place	Indoors
Players	10 to 20
Time	20 to 30 Minutes
Energy	Minimal

Create your own version of this popular television game show. Choose questions (or in this case, answers) that are appropriate for your group, and let the fun begin!

EQUIPMENT

- Stopwatch, or watch with second hand
- Prepared gameboard to hang on the wall, with accompanying answer sheet for the emcee. To make the board, use a piece of poster board, which has a 25 square grid marked off. Above each column, write the name of the category. Then, in each of the squares under it, write the answers to questions related to that topic, having them get progressively harder as you go down the column. Cover each square with a slip of paper on which is written \$100, \$200, \$300, \$400, \$500, progressively down each topic's column. Under any one of these covers, put a second slip which says "Daily Double."

FORMATION

Seat players close together, approximately 6 to 10 feet from the opposite team, near the playing board. One person from each team should be appointed as the team's spokesperson. Only he/she may give an answer to the emcee.

TO PLAY

With due pomp and circumstance, the emcee should review the rules of the game. (Then everyone should "sing" the Jeopardy theme song!) One team is selected to begin. They may chose any square to begin. The emcee removes the tag covering that answer, and reads it aloud. That team has ten seconds to come up with its most appropriate question. The team captain *only* may give the teams response to the emcee. If they correctly identify the question, their team is awarded that score. (Adhere that tag to the wall on the side of the board that their team is on.) If they are unable to correctly identify the question, the opposing team gets 5 seconds to make a guess and win the points. If neither team gives the correct response, neither team gets the points.

Alternate between teams for turns, if your questions are pretty easy, to avoid a "run away" game. With tougher questions, play moves back and forth between teams, depending on which team supplied the correct response. You will have to judge which is most appropriate for your own situation.

Play continues until all the "answers" have been "questioned." Tally up the scores for each team from the tags you have adhered to the wall in front of each team. Be sure to award a double value to the tag which had "Daily Double" under it. Present the victors with their winnings: play money totaling their score! And everyone waves good-bye to the studio audience while they all sing, "Ba-da-da-dum, Ba-da-dum..."

Trivia-Tac-Toe

Place	Indoors
Players	10 to 20
Time	10 to 15 Minutes
Energy	Minimal

This game combines the individual challenge of answering trivia questions with the team effort of winning human tic-tac-toe. Try it!

EQUIPMENT

- Prepared list of trivia questions (or get a set of Trivial Pursuit™ cards)
- Pencil and paper to keep track of the score
- Masking or duct tape to mark off a 9 foot by 9 foot tic-tac-toe board on the floor

FORMATION

Two teams should line up single file, with about 6 to 10 feet of space separating the two teams. The leader should stand in front of the two lines, and the tic-tac-toe "board" marked off by tape should be off to the side about 10 feet.

TO PLAY

The leader gives a trivia question to the first player on one team. He, and he alone, may answer the question. If he does so successfully, he may take a spot on one of the tic-tac-toe squares. (Use colored arm bands to distinguish teams; or have one team sit in a square, and have the other team stand.) If the player cannot answer his question, he moves to the end of his team's line, and the same question is given to the first player on the opposing team. If she correctly answers the question, she may take a place on the tic-tac-toe board. If she cannot, she moves to the back of her team's line. Either way, the next new question is given to the second team.

Each correct answer earns that player's team one point. If a team successfully places players three in a row on the tic-tac-toe board, the team wins an additional 5 points. After a successful tic-tac-toe, or when all 9 spaces on the board are full, those players return to the end of their team's lines.

Play continues until one team reaches a predetermined score, or you run out of trivia questions!

For a variation, ask questions that reinforce school lessons, or directly apply to something the group is learning or familiar with, such as multiplication tables, or history facts.

Place	Indoors
Players	8 to 16
Time	20 to 30 Minutes
Energy	Minimal

Go To The Head Of The Room

Remember playing the board game "Go To The Head Of The Class" as a kid? This game is a take-off on that, only it adds an element of creativity: the group makes up their own life-sized game board!

EQUIPMENT

- Large stack of 8 1/2 x 11 inch scrap paper
- Markers or crayons for the group
- Die (one dice)
- Prepared list of educational or trivia questions (with answer sheet)

PREPARATION

Give each person 3 or 4 blank sheets of paper and a marker. Have them write directions on them similar to ones found on game boards (e.g., move ahead 3 spaces; lose 1 turn; roll again, etc.). When those are written, take them (and many blank ones) and lay out a winding pathway across the room. You may want to include some shortcuts, too!

TO PLAY

Line up the players behind the starting line. Make a list of the order in which they are standing, so you can keep track of whose turn it is throughout the game. Ask the first person in line a question from your list. If she answers it correctly, she may roll the die and advance that number of spaces. If the square on which she lands says something, she should follow those directions before the next player has a turn. If a player cannot correctly answer his first question, he returns to the back of the line. In subsequent turns, a player who cannot answer a question merely remains in position, and does not roll the die. Continue asking players questions and allowing them to roll and move along the game board until someone makes it to the head of the room. Ceremoniously crown them the winner. Maybe even give them a light bulb for being so bright!

VARIATION

To keep the game lighthearted, include some wacky directions along with the trivia or educational questions. See the game *Ridiculous Requests Relay* (page 133) for some sample cards.

Inflated Interests

Place	Indoors
Players	10 to 30
Time	10 to 15 Minutes
Energy	Minimal

Developed by an aspiring Air Force pilot student of mine, this is a nice exercise to do as your group gets to know each other.

EQUIPMENT

- White 9" balloons, enough for one per person, plus extras
- Several broad tipped permanent markers

FORMATION

Ask your group to sit in a large circle, so everyone can see everyone else. Hand each person a balloon.

TO PLAY

On their inflated balloon, each person should draw two or three pictures which represent something significant in their lives. (This should be done without anyone else watching them.) Hobbies, pets, significant others, and aspirations might be the subjects of their pictures, for example. Once everyone has finished drawing on their balloons, everyone tosses them into the center of the circle, and selects a different one. At this point, you may want to pull the circle of people in tighter together, so it is easier to see and hear one another. In turn, each person interprets the pictures on the balloon he has selected, and speculates who it represents. If he is incorrect in his guess, he may make one or two more guesses before the real artist identifies herself. When a person's balloon is correctly identified, she may take a minute to explain what the pictures are, and why they are significant to her. Continue around the circle, until all the guessers and artists have had a turn.

Place	Indoors/Outdoors
Players	16 or More
Time	10 to 15 Minutes
Energy	Minimal

Kentucky Derby

It's a horse race! It's a trivia game! It's both! It's Kentucky Derby!

EQUIPMENT

- List of trivia questions, with answers
- Masking tape to mark off race lanes

FORMATION

Divide your group into teams of 8 to 10. Each team should select players to serve as a horse, a jockey, and as the answer runner. The rest of their team will remain seated in a group, answering the questions. Situate the teams in a semicircle around the leader, at a distance of approximately 15 feet. Masking tape race lanes should be laid out behind the leader. Strips of tape should be placed crossways every two feet, so the horses and jockeys can advance one square at a time along the raceway to the finish line. Have the horses and jockeys line up at the "Starting Gate" to begin the game.

TO PLAY

The leader reads a question to all the teams. Teammates quickly confer, and send their runner up to the leader with their answer. The first team to give the correct answer may have their horse and jockey advance one space closer to the finish line.

"It's neck 'n neck, folks, as they approach the finish line! And the winner is . . . " (the first one across, of course!)

Team Pin The Tail On The Donkey

Place	Indoors
Players	Any Number
Time	10 to 15 Minutes
Energy	Minimal

This game isn't always "quiet." In fact, it can get downright noisy! It's the most exciting way to play Pin the Tail on the Donkey I've ever seen!

EQUIPMENT

- Bandana or blindfold per team
- A poster of a tail-less donkey, with "X" marking the target spot
- A "tail" per team
- Masking tape
- Paper and marker for score keeping

FORMATION

Divide your group into two or three teams, and line them up approximately 15 feet from the wall on which the donkey poster is mounted.

TO PLAY

Blindfold the first person on each team, and hand them a donkey tail. In turn, spin the player around three times, and head him in the general direction of the donkey. Repeat this with the other blindfolded players, then let them remove their eye coverings, and see how they did. Award 3 points for the tail closest to the target "X," 2 for the next closest, 1 for farthest away. Remove the tails from the poster, and hand them to the next players. Blindfold the next wave of contestants, and let them have a turn. Rotate which team's contestant goes first, so all teams have an equal advantage/handicap. After everyone has had a turn, total up the score to determine the winner.

Place	Indoors
Players	Any Number
Time	5 Minutes
Energy	Minimal

Backward/ Forward

Here's a simple pencil and paper game to challenge your group!

EQUIPMENT

- Pencil and paper for each player

TO PLAY

Distribute pencils and paper to each player, as they sit on the floor or at a table. Tell them they have 3 minutes to come up with as many words as they can that spell a word frontwards and backwards. For example, NAP/PAN, and TOP/POT would work, as would MOM or TOT. At the end of the given time, let several people read off their lists, and see how everyone did.

Laugh Lines

Place	Indoors/Outdoors
Players	20 or More
Time	5 Minutes
Energy	Minimal

Laugh Lines is a game of conquest—of the funniest kind!

EQUIPMENT

- Stopwatch, or watch with second hand

FORMATION

Divide your team in half. (See Chapter 3 for creative ways to do this.) Have the two teams line up opposite each other, at a distance of about 3 feet.

TO PLAY

Select one team to go first. They then have 30 seconds to try to make someone, anyone, from the other team smile or laugh. If they are successful, the guilty laughers come across the line, and become part of the other team. After 30 seconds, the other team has a turn at trying to lure their opponents into laughter. Continue for several rounds, seeing which team can get and keep the most players.

Place	Indoors
Players	Any Number
Time	5 Minutes
Energy	Minimal

Where In The U.S. Are The Craters Of The Moon?

Well-known as well as somewhat obscure units of the National Park system are the subject of this trivia game. See how many your group knows. Say, where is Craters of the Moon National Monument, anyway?!

EQUIPMENT

- Prepared sheet and pencil for each player

TO PLAY

Listed below are National Park Service Units located in the United States. In the blank next to each, write the state in which it is located.

Acadia National Park (*Maine*)
Assateague Island National Seashore (*Maryland*)
Big Bend National Park (*Texas*)
Cape Cod National Seashore (*Massachusetts*)
Crater Lake National Park (*Oregon*)
Craters of the Moon National Monument (*Idaho*)
Denali National Park (*Alaska*)
Dinosaur National Monument (*Utah and Colorado*)
Everglades National Park (*Florida*)
Fire Island National Seashore (*New York*)
Glacier National Park (*Montana*)
Grand Canyon National Park (*Arizona*)
Great Smoky Mountains National Park (*Tennessee and North Carolina*)
Hot Springs National Park (*Arkansas*)
Ice Age National Scientific Reserve (*Wisconsin*)
Mammoth Cave National Park (*Kentucky*)
Mount Rushmore National Memorial (*South Dakota*)
Olympic National Park (*Washington*)
Sleeping Bear Dunes National Lakeshore (*Michigan*)
Teddy Roosevelt National Memorial (*North Dakota*)
Voyageurs National Park (*Minnesota*)
White Sands National Monument (*New Mexico*)
Yellowstone National Park (*Wyoming*)
Yosemite National Park (*California*)
Zion National Park (*Utah*)

Vacation Venture

Place	Indoors
Players	8 to 24
Time	20 to 30 Minutes
Energy	Minimal

Here's a way to get to take that cross-country trip you've been wanting to make—without the expenses! Groups map out a route, and progress along it by answering questions correctly. As with real vacations, your group may enjoy Vacation Venture so much, they won't want to go home!

EQUIPMENT

- U.S. road maps, one per team
- Highlighter markers, one per team
- Miniature toy cars, one per team
- Rulers and pencils, one per team
- Deck of Vacation Venture cards, which you need to make up in advance

PREPARATION

To prepare Vacation Venture cards, get a package of 3" x 5" cards. On one side, write a trivia or educational question appropriate for your group. Number these cards on a corner, and write the number with corresponding answer on a master answer sheet. On a dozen or more cards, write travel-related situations with corresponding commands, and shuffle them together with the Vacation Venture cards. These situations might include things such as:

"Road construction. Only cover 50 miles today."
"Drank some bad water. Lose a turn while you recover."
"Beautiful driving weather today. Advance an extra 100 miles."
"Left your wallet at the campground last night. Go back to get it."
"Rest area closed for renovations. Hurry 50 miles to the next one."

TO PLAY

Divide your group into teams of 3 or 4. Give each group a map, marker, ruler, pencil, and car—and 5 minutes to decide where they want to go on vacation. The routes they map out with the highlighter must be at least 2000 miles in length, using the map's scale. With pencil and ruler, the team should mark lines across the highlighted path, at 50 mile intervals. (You may also make up your own scale, one inch equals 50 miles, if that is simpler. All teams should use the same scale.)

When each team's route is mapped out, the game may begin. Each team places their car on your present location. In turn, the leader takes a Vacation Venture card off the stack, and reads the question to the first team. If they can correctly answer it within 10 seconds, they may advance their car 100 miles. If they fail to answer correctly, they must remain where they are until their next turn. If a Vacation Venture card is drawn with a travel-related situation on it, follow the directions given. Teams continue taking turns until one team successfully makes it home.

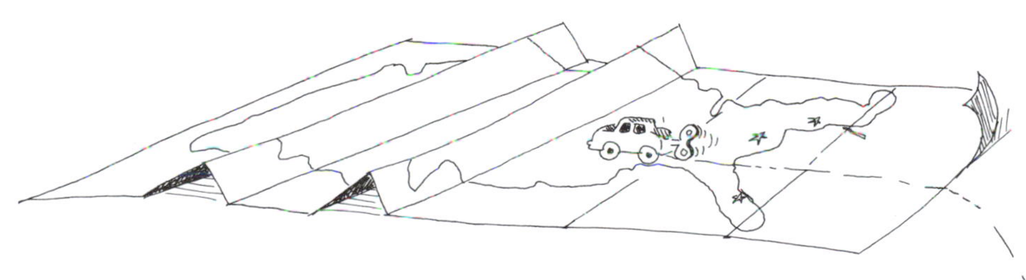

Some Final Thoughts

I've filled your head with lots of information and, I hope, some good ideas. In the first chapter, we reviewed the importance and qualities of effective recreation activity leaders. We took a look at planning for your participants, and at planning recreation activity programs in Chapter 2. In Chapter 3, I shared with you a variety of practical pointers for presenting activities, and for organizing participants. Chapters 4-8 presented over 130 activities (from challenging to crazy!) for you to try.

Two sections of this book are still before you: References and Resources, and the Game Finder. As you look over the list of books in the References and Resources section, you will notice some are rather new publications, while others are quite old. Both were valuable to me for ideas and for inspiration. You should find them useful as well. I am particularly excited about the Game Finder. Designed to assist you in selecting appropriate activities for your group, the Game Finder is a "quick glance" activities overview and index. The Game Finder is a resource for *you,* so feel free to highlight games you like, make notes in the margins, or add your own ideas at the end. It is my hope that this whole book becomes a valued and frequently used tool in your activities supply chest, and not merely another entry on your reference shelf.

Yes, this book is ending, but in a way, it is beginning, too. Once you have finished reading through it, you can begin using it. You can take the material presented here, and put it into practice. You can try out the ideas and activities on your group, and see what works for you. Most importantly, you can make a difference in people's lives: by caring about them, by affirming their worth, and by bringing people closer together.

So close this book, make a plan, grab some people, and get out there and have some FUN TIMES!

References And Resources

Barry, S. A. (1987). *The World's Best Party Games.* New York, NY: Sterling Publishing Company, Inc.

Eisenberg, H., and Eisenberg, L. (1949). *The Pleasure Chest.* Nashville, TN: Partheon Press.

Eisenberg, H., and Eisenberg, L. (1951). *The Family Pleasure Chest.* Nashville, TN: Partheon Press.

Eisenberg, H., and Eisenberg, L. (1954). *How to Help Folks Have Fun.* New York, NY: Association Press.

Eisenberg, H., and Eisenberg, L. (1956). *The Omnibus of Fun.* New York, NY: Association Press.

Fluegelman, A. (1976). *The New Games Book.* New York, NY: Headlands Press.

Fluegelman, A. (1981). *More New Games.* New York, NY: Dolphin Books/Doubleday and Company, Inc.

Group Publishing. (1988). *Quick Crowdbreakers and Games for Youth Groups.* Loveland, CO: Group Books.

Harbin, E. O. (1968). *The Fun Encyclopedia.* New York, NY: Abingdon Press.

Harris, F. (1976). *Games.* Detroit, MI: Published by author.

Macfarlan, A. (1952). *New Games for 'Tween-Agers.* New York, NY: Association Press.

Mason, B., and Mitchell, E. (1935). *Social Games for Recreation.* New York, NY: A. S. Barnes and Company, Inc.

National Recreation Association. (1950). *Recreation Activities for Adults.* New York, NY: Association Press.

Orlick, T. (1982). *The Second Cooperative Sports and Games Book.* New York, NY: Pantheon Books.

Rice, W. (1986). *Great Ideas for Small Youth Groups.* Grand Rapids, MI: Zondervan Publishing House.

Rice, W. (1989). *Up Close & Personal: How to Build Community in Your Youth Group.* Grand Rapids, MI: Zondervan Publishing House.

Rice, W., and Yaconelli, M. (1982). *Incredible Ideas for Youth Groups.* Grand Rapids, MI: Zondervan Publishing House.

Rice, W., and Yaconelli, M. (1986). *Play It!* Grand Rapids, MI: Zondervan Publishing House.

Rohnke, K. (1977). *Cowstails & Cobras: A guide to Ropes Courses, Initiative Games, and other Adventure Activities.* Hamilton, MA: Project Adventure, Inc.

Rohnke, K. (1984). *Silver Bullets.* Hamilton, MA: Project Adventure, Inc.

Rydberg, D. (1985). *Building Community in Youth Groups.* Loveland, CO: Group Books.

Wood, C., and Goddard, G. (1938). *The Complete Book of Games.* Garden City, NY: Garden City Books.

Yaconelli, M., and Rice, W. (1986). *Creative Socials & Special Events.* Grand Rapids, MI: Zondervan Publishing House.

Yaconelli, M., and Rice, W. (1986). *Super Ideas for Youth Groups.* Grand Rapids, MI: Zondervan Publishing House.

Game Finder

The Game Finder has been designed to assist you in selecting appropriate activities for your group. A quick glance at the grid will give you an overview of the main elements of each activity—which is especially helpful when you have limited preparation time!

KEY

Place

Indoors—Check individual games to determine size of facility needed.
Outdoors—Large, open, outdoor area, such as a playing field
W—Wooded outdoor area
Ind./Out.—game works equally well indoors or outdoors

Number of Players

Numbers given are guidelines. Slightly larger or smaller groups might suffice.

Time

Time requirements given are approximate. In the case of Group Starters, individual time is given. More time may be required for the entire group to participate.

Level of Energy

Minimal = No running necessary (also includes seated activities)
Moderate = Some running/moving
Maximum = High energy output required

Special Preparation

Special preparation is required to present this activity.

Page

Indicates the page on which activity is described.

GROUP STARTERS

Group Starters	Place			Number of Players	Time (Min.)	Energy			Special Prep	Page
	Indoors	Outdoors	Ind./Out.			Minimal	Moderate	Maximum		
Bubble Blowing Contest	●			Any #	As Avail.	●				23
Caption Writing Contest	●			Any #	As Avail.	●			●	16
Coin Toss	●			Any #	As Avail.	●			●	25
Duel			●	2/More	As Avail.		●			26
Face Up Card Toss	●			Any #	As Avail.	●				17
Nature I.D.			●	Any #	As Avail.	●			●	21
Nose Knows, The	●			Any #	As Avail.	●			●	18
Penny Pondering	●			Any #	5	●			●	27
Pin A Pal	●			Pairs	As Avail.		●			28
Scrambled Valentines	●			Any #	5	●			●	24
Seed I.D.			●	Any #	As Avail.	●			●	22
Taste Tasters			●	Any #	As Avail.	●			●	19

MIXERS

Mixers	Place			Number of Players	Time (Min.)	Energy			Special Prep	Page
	Indoors	Outdoors	Ind./Out.			Minimal	Moderate	Maximum		
Allow Me To Introduce To You...			●	12 to 24	10 to 15	●				35
Blown Up Blender	●			16/More	5		●		●	44
Deal The Deck	●			20/More	5		●			50
"Do This" Mixer			●	Any #	5	●				43
Getting-To-Know-You Backrubs			●	Any #	20 to 30	●			●	36
Group Juggling			●	10 to 35	5	●				33
Guess The Guest	●			16 to 30	20 to 30	●				51
Human Taco	●			18/More	5		●		●	45
Human Twister	●			15 to 30	5	●			●	32
I Say, It's A Beautiful Day!			●	12 to 24	5	●				38
I'm Going To Montana			●	12 to 24	5	●				39
Laugh Pass			●	12 to 24	5	●				40
Mud Tub Treasure Hunt			●	Any #	20 to 30		●		●	49
Mystery Mingler, The			●	20/More	5	●			●	34
Name Toss			●	8 to 20	5	●				30
Newspaper Delivery	●			24/More	5			●		41
Newspaper Puzzler	●			18 to 30	5	●			●	42
Pet Peeve Pass			●	10 to 30	5	●				31
Pick A Partner	●			12 to 40	5	●				46
Ping			●	Any #	10 to 15		●		●	48
Yarn Game, The	●			Any #	5		●		●	47

TEAM BUILDERS

Team Builders	Place			Number of Players	Time (Min.)	Energy			Special Prep	Page
	Indoors	Outdoors	Ind./Out.			Minimal	Moderate	Maximum		
Cooperative Bean Bag Toss			●	4/More	5	●				64
Cooperative Snacking	●			8 to 15	10 to 15		●			65
Don't Axe Me!			●	5 to 8	10 to 15			●		60
Evacuation		●		8 to 16	20 to 30		●			56
Group Rope Jumping			●	10 to 35	5		●			54
People Movers			●	8 to 12	10 to 15		●			67
Queen Of Sheba		●		5 to 8	5		●			59
Siamese Centipede			●	6 to 8	5		●			66
Spaghetti Structures	●			9 to 18	10 to 15	●				62
Team Challenge Obstacle Course			●	6 to 12	10 to 15			●		55
Teetering Team		●		10 to 25	5		●			58
Through The Hoop	●			8 to 15	5		●			61
Tube Trip			●	6 to 15	10 to 15		●			63

AFFIRMATION ACTIVITIES

Affirmation Activities	Place			Number of Players	Time (Min.)	Energy			Special Prep	Page
	Indoors	Outdoors	Ind./Out.			Minimal	Moderate	Maximum		
Affirmation Fold-Ups	●			Any #	5	●				70
Affirmation Web			●	Any #	10 to 15	●				71
Bumper Stickers	●			Any #	10 to 15	●			●	74
Gifts			●	10 to 20	10 to 15	●				73
M&M® Mentions			●	Any #	5	●				69
Opinion Game			●	Any #	5		●			72
Qualities Inventory	●			12 to 24	10 to 15	●				75
Secret Stickers	●			Any #	10 to 15	●			●	76
Self Sculptures			●	6 to 24	10 to 15	●				77
Shirt Of Arms	●			6 to 24	20 to 30	●			●	78
Thanksgiving Envelopes	●			Any #	10 to 15	●				80
Valentine Exchange	●			12 to 24	10 to 15	●			●	79

ACTIVE GAMES

Active Games	Place			Number of Players	Time (Min.)	Energy			Special Prep	Page
	Indoors	Outdoors	Ind./Out.			Minimal	Moderate	Maximum		
12 Minute Kickball			●	18 to 40	10 to 15			●		86
4-Way Balloon Bust Up	●			32 to 60	10 to 15			●		103
A.T.B. (All Touch Ball)			●	16 to 30	20 to 30			●		97
Balloon Batting Battle	●			16 to 50	20 to 30			●		105
Bandana Ball			●	12/More	5		●		●	104
Beat The Ball			●	10 to 25	5		●			96
Black Panther		● W		8 to 15	20 to 30		●			94
Bronco Tag			●	20/More	10 to 15			●		83
Defend De Fruit			●	Pairs	5		●			101
Frisbee™ Baseball			●	20 to 30	20 to 30		●			88
Kickball For All			●	20 to 40	20 to 30		●			84
Lumberjack Contest	●			20/More	20 to 30+			●	●	108
Mat Ball			●	20 to 40	20 to 30		●			87
Poison Papers			●	20/More	5			●		106
Potato Poaching			●	12 to 24	5		●			107
Pull Over			●	Any #	5			●		100
Rescue Rudolph Snowball Fight	●			20 to 40	10 to 15		●			89
Ribbon Rip-Off			●	Any #	5			●		91
Samurai Soda Swatters			●	12 to 30	10 to 15		●			99
Secret Summons		● W		10 to 20	20 to 30		●			93
Steal The Broom Hockey			●	12 to 20	20 to 30		●			95
Swat			●	12/More	10 to 15		●			92
Taunt The Tiger			●	12 to 24	5		●			102
Wall Ball	●			12 to 24	10 to 15		●			82

RELAYS

Relays	Place			Number of Players	Time (Min.)	Energy			Special Prep	Page
	Indoors	Outdoors	Ind./Out.			Minimal	Moderate	Maximum		
52 Card Pick Up	●			12/More	5			●		140
Antarctic Adventure	●			12/More	5		●		●	127
Balloon Batting Relay	●			12/More	5			●		123
Balloon Blow Up	●			12/More	5		●			121
Balloon Sweep Relay	●			12/More	5			●		124
Bandana Balance	●			16/More	5		●			141
Bombs Away!	●			16/More	5		●		●	144
Caterpillar Obstacle Course			●	16/More	5		●		●	117
Chariot Races	●			12/More	5			●		115
Chicken In Every Pot	●			16/More	5	●				139
Cocoon The Platoon			●	16/More	5		●			116
Domino Relay	●			12/More	5		●			113
Duck Waddle Relay	●			12/More	5		●			122
Elastic Band Relay			●	12/More	5			●	●	131
Face To Face	●			20/More	5		●			146
Hoop Hop Relay			●	16/More	5			●		126
Inheritance			●	16/More	5			●	●	132
Jump Rope Relay			●	12/More	5			●		120
Licorice Lunacy Race			●	16/More	5			●		143
Motley Medley			●	12/More	5		●		●	137
Pepsi® Pass			●	16/More	5		●			138
Potato Pass	●			28 to 60	5			●		125

Continued on next page

RELAYS (Continued)

Relays	Place			Number of Players	Time (Min.)	Energy			Special Prep	Page
	Indoors	Outdoors	Ind./Out.			Minimal	Moderate	Maximum		
Raisinet® Racing			●	20/More	5		●			145
Recycling Rangers Relay			●	12/More	10 to 15		●		●	118
Ridiculous Request Relay			●	20/More	10 to 15		●		●	133
Sleigh Ride	●			12/More	5			●		114
Space Shuttle Shuffle, The			●	16/More	5			●		128
Spear The Sweets			●	12/More	5		●			130
Spelling Relay	●			12/More	5		●		●	135
Spike 'n Strut			●	12/More	5			●		119
Sunbathers Relay			●	12/More	5			●		112
Swallowing Goldfish			●	16/More	10 to 15		●			142
Whisper Down The Raceway			●	12/More	5			●	●	129
Wobble Ball Relay			●	20/More	5			●	●	136

QUIET GAMES

Quiet Games	Place			Number of Players	Time (Min.)	Energy			Special Prep	Page
	Indoors	Outdoors	Ind./Out.			Minimal	Moderate	Maximum		
Airplane Adventure	●			8 to 16	10 to 15	●			●	161
Backward/Forward	●			Any #	5	●				171
"Brussels Sprouts/Peanut Butter"			●	Any #	As Avail.	●				150
Confused Cats	●			Any #	5	●			●	155
Go To The Head Of The Room	●			8 to 16	20 to 30	●			●	167
Inflated Interests	●			10 to 30	10 to 15	●				168
Jeopardy	●			10 to 20	20 to 30	●			●	164
Kentucky Derby			●	16/More	10 to 15	●			●	169
Laugh Lines			●	20/More	5	●				172
Match 'em	●			10 to 20	20 to 30	●				162
Nutty Questionnaire	●			Any #	5	●			●	156
Personalities	●			8 to 12	20 to 30	●				151
Ridiculous Responses	●			Any #	5	●				153
State Stars	●			6 to 15	10 to 15	●			●	154
"Take Me Out To The Mall, Mom"			●	Any #	As Avail.	●				150
Tanks			●	12 to 24	10 to 15	●			●	148
Team Pin The Tail On The Donkey	●			Any #	10 to 15	●			●	170
Toothpick Mind Pricks	●			Any #	10 to 15	●			●	157
Trivia Tac Toe	●			10 to 20	10 to 15	●			●	166
Vacation Venture	●			8 to 24	20 to 30	●			●	174
Where In The U.S. Are The Craters Of The Moon?	●			Any #	5	●			●	173

Related Books from Venture Publishing

The Activity Gourmet
by Peggy Powers

Great Special Events and Activities
by Annie Morton, Angie Prosser and Sue Spangler

Leisure Education: A Manual of Activities and Resources
by Norma J. Stumbo and Steven R. Thompson

Leisure Education II: More Activities and Resources
by Norma J. Stumbo

Recreation Programming And Activities For Older Adults
by Jerold E. Elliott and Judith A. Sorg-Elliott

Venture Publishing, Inc
1999 Cato Avenue
State College, PA 16801
814-234-4561